P9-BYH-366

A WILDERNESS CALLED
GRAND CANYON

Stewart Aitchison

Foreword by Jim Ruch
Featuring the photography of Dick Dietrich

VOYAGEUR PRESS

For Ann and Kate

Copyright © 1991 by Stewart Aitchison

Printed in Hong Kong through Bookbuilders Ltd.
91 92 93 94 95 5 4 3 2 1

Library of Congress Cataloging-in-Publication Data
Aitchison, Stewart W.
   A wilderness called Grand Canyon / Stewart Aitchison.
      p.   cm.
   Includes bibliographic references.
   ISBN 0-89658-149-7
   1. Natural history—Arizona—Grand Canyon. I. Title.
   QH105.A65A38   1991
508.791′32—dc20   90-25373
                                                      CIP

Published by
Voyageur Press, Inc.
P.O. Box 338
123 North Second Street
Stillwater, MN 55082 U.S.A.
In Minn 612-430-2210
Toll-free 800-888-9653

Voyageur Press books are also available at discounts for quantities for educational, fundraising, premium, or sales-promotion use. For details contact the marketing department. Please write or call for our free catalog of natural history publications.

CONTENTS

The secretive gray fox makes its home in the Grand Canyon and much of the United States. (Photo © by Stewart Aitchison.)

FOREWORD

The Grand Canyon is so perfectly named, and yet so widely and commonly known, that we frequently pronounce the words without the emphasis that the reality of the canyon deserves. To see it in person, however, still takes the breath away. To become immersed in it—over the edge on a back-country trail, tossed in a raft by a Colorado River rapid, or silently counting down the terraces of geologic time while watching the sun set from our own private pinnacle along the rim—is to realize what a wonder we are privileged to behold.

In *A Wilderness Called Grand Canyon,* Stewart Aitchison has combined an introduction to the canyon, for those visitors who have a brief time to see this special place, with a tantalizing overview of the history, the values, the facts, and the mysteries that have inspired lifetimes of human endeavor and contemplation.

As you read and share glimpses of the vast and complex natural system that makes up the Grand Canyon, you'll come to understand the special feelings people have for this place. From the creation myths of Native Americans to the excitement of President Teddy Roosevelt when

he declared it a National Monument, the canyon calls for more than superlatives. It inspires awe.

Thus it is all the more horrifying to realize that, once again, the insatiable technological demands of our society are endangering our natural inheritance. In the midst of describing the remarkable values you will find in the canyon, Aitchison also tells of the threats to its future. The stack gases from coal-fired power plants are befouling its superb views. Just upstream the single-minded operation of Glen Canyon Dam—to maximize peaking electrical power— is creating huge daily fluctuations in the flow of the Colorado River, destroying beaches, impacting the canyon's riparian ecosystem, and jeopardizing the existence of endangered fish.

The merit of this book is that it helps a newcomer understand and appreciate the full scope of what exists in the Grand Canyon. It also reminds those who know the canyon well, and return often, of the many wonders they cherish and the great wilderness to be preserved.

—JIM RUCH, *Executive Vice President, Grand Canyon Trust,* Flagstaff, Arizona

Across from Nankoweap Canyon, looking southwest. (Photo © by S. Aitchison.)

A WORLD IN ITSELF

Why another book on the Grand Canyon? Like the canyon itself, the body of literature describing and extolling the great canyon is vast. Yet, except for field guides and geologic explanations, few works written for laypeople deal with the natural history, primarily biology, of the Grand Canyon.

Not that there hasn't been a great deal of scientific research done. Rest assured that there has been and continues to be investigation into many different aspects of the canyon's natural history, from basics to esoterics: studies as diverse as "The Ecology and Natural History of Ants of Grand Canyon" to "Off-site Radiation Exposure Review Project (ORERP); Dose Assessment in the Extended Region (U3O3 data from GC Sample Sites)"; as abstruse as "Intrinsic Oxygen Fugacity Measurements of Mantle Derived Xenoliths from Vulcan's Throne, Arizona: A Study of the Retox Conditions in the Earth's Mantle" to relatively applicable ones such as "Impacts of Timber Harvest and Fire on Populations of the Tassel-Eared Squirrel on the North Kaibab Plateau, Arizona."

Unfortunately, most of this fascinating knowledge is buried in technical reports and scientific journals where the jargon of science often intimidates the casual natural history buff. The average visitor to the Grand Canyon leaves unaware of the exciting discoveries being made by scientists in many different fields—bald eagle studies, the impact of air pollution, the effect of Glen Canyon Dam on the inner canyon's ecology, the evolution of the canyon landscape. Geologists, biologists, archaeologists, and others are working individually and in consort to gain a deeper understanding of this wonderful canyon wilderness.

This book attempts to reveal a little of the canyon's remarkable natural history. The emphasis is on the plants and animals that live in this unique place, although I would be remiss if I didn't discuss a little of the area's geology as well as the human component of the Grand Canyon's ecosystem. A bit of historical background is also given, along with the results of some recent and current studies.

This book is *not* a trail guide, although I do recount a few adventures and misadventures into the canyon. For those who wish to explore the trails and byways (an activity I wholeheartedly endorse for the fit and experienced), a number of good guidebooks are available.

For hiking I recommend Harvey Butchart's *Grand Canyon Treks*. Butchart now has three volumes in this series, each one chock full of little-known routes and historical notes. But be aware that he is a master of understatement; an easy trip for Butchart could turn out to be an epic adventure for you. Better for the novice canyon hiker is Scott Thybony's booklet *A Guide to Hiking the Inner Canyon,* which covers

A claret cup hedgehog cactus blooms on the rim of Havasu Canyon, the canyon home of the Havasupai people. (Photo © by S. Aitchison.)

the more popular trails, and my own *A Naturalist's Guide to Hiking the Grand Canyon,* which offers suggestions for exploration in more remote areas.

For the motorist, *Along the Rim* by Nancy Loving is a beautiful booklet describing the history and scenes along the South Rim.

The river runner will find Larry Stevens's waterproof edition of *The Colorado River in Grand Canyon: A Guide* indispensable for a whitewater trip through the Grand Canyon.

Nor is my book a field guide for identifying things. For those of you who enjoy knowing the names of plants and animals, I would suggest Stephen Whitney's *A Field Guide to the Grand Canyon* as the only book that attempts to cover everything in one volume. For the avid naturalist, there are many other field guides specific to the Grand Canyon or to a particular group of plants or animals. Some of these are listed in the Further Reading section of this book.

For an entertaining and lucid overview of the Grand Canyon's geology, by far the best is Michael Collier's *An Introduction to Grand Canyon Geology.*

Back in 1957, Joseph Wood Krutch, a retired English professor turned naturalist, wrote *Grand Canyon: Today and all its yesterdays.* His delightful book popularized the canyon's natural history as it was understood at that time. I read and reread this book about a marvelous place known as the Grand Canyon. A spark of curiosity was ignited in the imagination of an impressionable youth stuck in the flatlands of the Midwest. Then when I was fourteen, my parents took me on a vacation trip to Arizona. As we drove north from Phoenix, each canyon that came into view sent my heart racing. "Is that it? Is that the Grand Canyon?"

My parents assured me that, no, we still had a long way to go. Off the side of Mingus Mountain we dropped into the Verde Valley toward the Red Rock Country surrounding Sedona. We followed along the bubbling Oak Creek, up tight switchbacks into majestic ponderosa pine forest, around the western base of the San Francisco Peaks, and out across flat, brush-covered plains where small herds of pronghorn browsed on sagebrush. *Where was that canyon?*

The road again passed through lovely open stands of pine. We paid the fee at the park entrance station, but still no awesome abyss could be detected. A few more miles and suddenly, quite without warning, the whole earth seemed to end.

I stood silently at Mather Point. Nothing, neither pictures nor words, can prepare you for that first view of the Grand Canyon. A warm, pine-scented breeze fanned that mental spark into a flame. I became consumed by the desire to learn more about this place, this raw, awesome wilderness called Grand Canyon.

Through this little volume, I wish to share with you a few gems of the canyon's extraordinary natural and human history and the forces challenging that unique place. Perhaps you will come to see the canyon as a living, evolving world, not just a huge, albeit astonishing, static rent in the earth's crust. As the nineteenth-century biologist C. Hart Merriam expressed it, "The Grand Canyon of the Colorado is a world in itself, and a great fund of knowledge is in store for the philosophic biologist whose privilege it is to study exhaustively the problems there presented."

The canyon has many lessons to teach us. My hope is that this book will serve as a stepping stone for the reader to reach greater paths of canyon knowledge and appreciation, and through that process, perhaps discover more about one's self.

Elves Chasm, River Mile 116.5. (Photo © by Ralph Lee Hopkins, Wilderland Images.)

FIRST VIEWS

On a typical first visit to Grand Canyon National Park, you'll probably approach the Grand Canyon via the South Rim (the most easily accessible side), as nearly four million other visitors do each year. Your initial view of the canyon, then, will most likely be from Mather Point, the first main scenic turnout beyond the South Rim Entrance Station. On this particular summer day, as on most summer days, the parking lot at this view point is jammed. Recreational vehicles and tour buses butt end to end, rows of cars overflow their designated spaces, and throngs of camera-wielding tourists stand cheek-to-jowl snapping photos in the glare of the midday sun. It's hard to say which is more overwhelming, the Grand Canyon or the crowd at Mather Point.

The viewpoint was named for Stephen Mather, an influential, wealthy industrial leader, who visited Grand Canyon National Monument and several other western national parks in 1914. (The Grand Canyon was designated as a national monument from 1908 until 1919, when congress established it as a national park.) Mather was dismayed at the lack of management he saw and fired off a letter of protest to Franklin K. Lane, Secretary of the Interior and, incidentally, an old college chum. Lane urged his friend to come to the Capitol and take charge of the park situation himself. Mather accepted the challenge. His new rank was Assistant to the Secretary. Two years later the National Park Service was founded with Mather as its first director. Up until that time the national parks had been "managed" by the forest service or, occasionally, the Army.

National Park Service Director Mather laid down a foundation for how our national parks should be developed and conserved for the future—a never-ending challenge, especially in light of our burgeoning population now evidenced by the masses that gather at the South Rim viewpoints.

For now, walk a short ways along the rim, away from the noisy majority at the point. While crowds tend to congregate at view points, most of the canyon is left in lonely majesty. Now you can concentrate on the landscape that, as Dr. Elliot Coues remarked in 1881, is ". . . the most wonderful crack of the ground in America."

Your park brochure reels off some extraordinary statistics: The canyon is approximately a mile deep, ranges from six hundred feet to eighteen miles in width, is over 277 miles long, and exposes rocks 1.7 billion years old. But these numbers pale in light of the awesome spectacle before you. Statistics cannot convey the intense emotional response felt by so many as they view this sight for the first time. Let your senses drink in the scene. Your first glimpse of the canyon can be numbing, inflicting you with a sense of disbelief. But be patient. The Grand Canyon

Overleaf: *The winter season can be a quiet time at the South Rim. (Photo © by Dick Dietrich.)*

takes time to comprehend, to fully appreciate. A landscape of such prodigious and incomparable proportions formed over millions of years cannot be absorbed in a few minutes.

Sure, there are deeper canyons such as those incredible barrancas in the Sierra Madre of northern Mexico. Some Southwest travelers declare the smaller scale and more intimate Oak Creek Canyon, south of Flagstaff, or Canyon de Chelly, in northeastern Arizona, more impressive, at least initially, because they are more "human-sized." And there are wider valleys and larger rivers than the Colorado. But the Grand Canyon combines elements of color, contour, and immensity like no other place on earth. The Grand Canyon is indeed unique.

If the canyon were a benign place, verdant with meadows and forest, watered with cool, bubbling streams, and easily accessible, its attraction would be more understandable. But it is not. The Grand Canyon is a big hole in the ground with horrid summer temperatures, very few springs, and knee-jarring, heart-pounding, perilous trails. I'm reminded of John Steinbeck's musing about another arid region—Baja California: "If it were lush and rich, one could understand the pull, but it is fierce and hostile and sullen."

Little wonder that in 1858 after a grueling trek to the canyon, Lieutenant Joseph Christmas Ives wrote in his *Report upon the Colorado River of the West:* "Ours has been the first, and will doubtless be the last, party of whites to visit this profitless locality. It seems intended by nature that the Colorado River, along the greater portion of its lonely and majestic way, shall be forever unvisited and undisturbed."

No one recorded what the very first visitor, probably a hunter searching for wild game some four thousand years ago, thought of this awesome spectacle. Even in 1540, when Captain García López de Cárdenas and his contingent of Spanish conquistadors, led by Hopi guides, encountered the rim near Desert View, the Spaniards apparently had little to say about the view. The journal kept by Pedro de Sotomayor, the official reporter on Cárdenas's trip to the canyon, has never been found. The only surviving account was written twenty years later by Pedro de Castañeda, who summed up the scene as a country "elevated and full of low twisted pines, very cold, and lying open to the north." We can surmise that the conquistadors were more interested in gold than in scenery. As Stephen J. Pyne wrote in his *Dutton's Point: An Intellectual History of the Grand Canyon:* "The Spanish mind was prepared to understand, and Spanish political economy prepared to assimilate, the discovery of golden Cibolas, not Grand Canyons. For Spain the Canyon was at best a hole, a vacuum of what was usable and assimilable, and at worst a disappointing barrier in the search for a maritime passage to the mythical Tenochtitlans and Cuzcos that, so rumor hinted, glistened in the interior [of North America]."

Major John Wesley Powell, the first to scientifically explore the Colorado River through the Grand Canyon in 1869, was one of the first literate persons to fully appreciate and attempt to write about the scenic wonders of the Grand Canyon. But Powell's protégé, Clarence Dutton, geologist, aesthete, writer, and soldier, wrote what many consider to be the greatest of all Grand Canyon books, *The Tertiary History of the Grand Canyon.* Dutton's geologic and geographic descriptions, couched in flowery, purple prose, have rarely been matched:

"I have in many places departed from the severe ascetic style which has become conventional in scientific monographs. Perhaps no apology is called for. Under ordinary circumstances the ascetic discipline is necessary. Give the imagination an inch and it is apt to take an ell, and the fundamental requirement of scientific method—accuracy of statement—is imperiled. But in the Grand Canyon district there is no such danger. The stimulants which are demoralizing elsewhere are necessary here to exalt the mind sufficiently to comprehend the sublimity of the subjects."

Accompanying the written word were often the works of artists who tried to capture their first view of the canyon's sublimity in oils, charcoal, and ink. Painter Thomas Moran was guided to the canyon by Powell in 1873, and the resulting canvas was purchased by Congress. Titled *Chasm of the Colorado,* the piece possesses the very power and spirit of the place. "In painting the Grand Canyon . . . I have to be full of my subject, I have to have knowledge. I must know the geology. I must know the rocks and trees and atmosphere. . . ." What Moran rendered from all this knowledge was not a photographic composition, but rather "an expression of the emotion" he experienced. "My personal scope is not realistic; all my tendencies are toward idealization."

Moran made a few illustrations which were included in Dutton's geologic monograph, but it was William Henry Holmes's works that have become the showpiece of report illustration. Holmes drew his view of the canyon with the critical eye of a scientist. His panoramic sketches reveal every contour with such clarity that a geologist can easily recognize each rock layer. Yet, the incredible preciseness of Holmes's drawings does not in any way diminish but instead adds to their aesthetic appeal.

As photography became more practical and photographic reproduction became possible, the elaborate descriptive style of prose and the use of illustrations became less fashionable. From photographer John Hillers, who accompanied Powell on his second Grand Canyon river trip in 1872, to the present-day point-and-shoot tourist, capturing the canyon on celluloid has been a favorite pastime.

Writers, artists, and photographers are not alone in their attempts to describe and understand the Grand Canyon. As Powell noted over a hundred years ago: "The wonders of the Grand Canyon cannot be adequately represented in symbols of speech, nor by speech itself. The resources of the graphic arts are taxed beyond their powers in attempting to portray its features. Language and illustration combined must fail. . . . It is the land of music."

One person who gazed into the canyon and heard music was composer Ferde Grofe. A series of visits in the 1920s led to a lifelong love affair with the Grand Canyon. In 1931, on a cold November evening in Chicago, Grofe's *Grand Canyon Suite* made its world premiere. Fellow composer Raymond Hubbell remarked, "God made it [the Grand Canyon] and He has given Ferde Grofe music to describe it."

In the early 1960s another composer, Paul Winters, came to the canyon. "[I] sat on the edge of the South Rim and played my soprano sax, and as the sound disappeared into the vastness, I imagined there must be spaces with wondrous echoes somewhere in the depths below me. But in those days I had no thought of making music in the wilderness." But subsequent trips, including three raft voyages, inspired Winters not only to write canyon music but to play and record some pieces within the canyon itself. The result is a recording titled *Canyon: A Celebration of the Grand Canyon.*

A few years ago, a hike into the canyon by harmonica virtuoso Robert Bonfiglio and flutist Clare Hoffman spawned an idea for the Grand Canyon Chamber Music Festival, which has now become a highly anticipated annual event at the South Rim. Concerts and recitals reflecting and celebrating the beauty and rhythm of nature are performed here each summer.

This wilderness called the Grand Canyon draws in the curious. The canyon inspires as it astounds. A myriad of people have attempted through language, art, music, and science to describe and understand this wondrous place. What better location for the naturalist to explore the riddles of the earth? Layers of rock, encompassing nearly half the earth's 4.5-billion-year history, lie exposed. Plant and animal communities that span from verdant evergreen forests to hostile, dry deserts are integrated upon the landscape. For thousands of years humans have roamed the inner canyon and have left their traces. A fascinating, intricate story of interconnected lives and evolutionary processes is slowly being unraveled by researchers. Take a few moments to listen to their story.

A WALK ALONG THE SOUTH RIM

On one of those wonderful, crisp fall days with a sky so blue that Easterners can't believe it's real, we turn off the East Rim Drive and head for the Moran Point Vista on the South Rim of the Grand Canyon. My wife Ann, daughter Kate, and I are off to hunt for bighorn sheep. No, not with a gun. Today we're armed only with binoculars and camera.

A tiny dark shape lumbers across the pavement. I slam on the brakes to avoid running over—a tarantula. A not uncommon sight during the autumn are dark brown, hairy tarantulas "migrating." Most of these traveling spiders are males who are not really migrating at all, but are on the prowl for a female.

I jump out of the car. As I approach the spider, he jerks to a stop and cautiously raises several of his legs (actually a few legs and two pedipalps, leglike appendages that help the male transfer sperm to the female). This somewhat intimidating position also exposes two large fangs jutting out from under the spider's cephalothorax. Though tarantulas possess eight eyes on top of their heads, their vision is restricted to barely perceiving light and shadow. Their sense of touch is very acute, however; hence the outstretched legs, ready to identify the approaching dark shape—me.

Gently, I scoop the spider up into my cupped hands and carry him to the side of road. Picking up a tarantula with one's bare hands generally causes alarm in nearby tourists, but this spider is much less venomous than the smaller black widow. Furthermore, although armed with those two curved fangs tipped with poison, tarantulas rarely bite humans. They prefer their regular prey of grasshoppers, cockroaches, caterpillars, scorpions, and other invertebrates. The powerful jaws of the tarantula mash the victim to a pulp as the digestive juices are regurgitated over it. The spider then sucks up its liquid meal.

Southwestern lore claims that the bite of the tarantula causes insanity. This view is probably a variation of the medieval European belief that the poison triggers tarantism, which is actually a nervous disorder. The victim's only "cure" was to dance to exhaustion. Of greater concern to me, however, are the tiny, venomous hairs that might rub off of the spider's upper abdomen. When inhaled, these urticating hairs can irritate mucous membranes, effectively deterring some predators.

Other predators are not so easily discouraged, however. An unfortunate spider may become parasitized by the large, black-bodied, orange-winged Pepsis wasp known as the tarantula hawk. The wasp delivers a paralyzing sting to the spider and then lays a single egg on the spider's body. When the egg hatches, the wasp larva eats its way out of the immobile but still living spider. To us squeamish humans the fate

Pinyon pine nuts were and still are an important food resource for Native Americans. (Photo © by Dick Dietrich.)

17

of the tarantula is perhaps a bit gruesome—but no one said survival was pretty.

If the migrating spider succeeds in avoiding wasps and cars and in locating a mate, his troubles are not yet over. Like some other spiders, the female tarantula may mistake the male for a meal rather than a lover. After the tryst, the male had better not linger too long if he doesn't want to become dessert. Next summer the female will deposit six to seven hundred eggs in a cocoon placed in the sun near the entrance to her burrow. Most of the baby spiders will die of starvation before reaching maturity; only a lucky few will reach the ripe old age of sixteen years or more.

We leave the tarantula to his search for a mate and resume our quest for bighorn sheep. After parking the car at the point, we shoulder our daypacks and stroll along the South Rim toward the New Hance Trail. The trail is new, however, only in the sense that it postdates the Old Hance Trail.

John Hance was a prospector who showed up at the Grand Canyon in 1883 to seek his fortune. Although gold and silver eluded him, he did manage to locate a small asbestos deposit in a canyon below Vishnu Temple on the north side of the Colorado River. To reach his prospects, Hance improved an ancient Indian route down what is now called Hance Canyon. In 1884, he guided Flagstaff businessman Edward Everett Ayer, Ayer's wife, and some of their friends to the bottom of the Grand Canyon. Later that year, other tourists literally followed in the Ayers' footsteps. Hance soon realized that there was more gold in the pockets of the tourists than in the walls of the Grand Canyon; therefore, he began to advertise himself as a canyon guide.

By 1894 his original route had been ravaged by rockslides, so Hance constructed a new trail down Red Canyon. The Red Canyon Trail is now known as the New Hance Trail.

Hance was a master storyteller. Leading his audience from a reasonable premise down a path of increasing fantasy, he entertained and informed canyon visitors. One visitor remarked,

"Captain John Hance—a genius, a philosopher, and a poet, the professor of a fund of information vastly important, if true. He laughs with the giddy, yarns to the gullible, talks to the sedate, and is a most excellent judge of scenery, human nature and pie. To see the Canyon only, and not to see Captain John Hance, is to miss half the show."

Hance sometimes boasted to his clients that he had dug the Grand Canyon. One day a little girl tugged on his sleeve and asked, "If you dug the canyon, what did you do with all that dirt?" Hance stroked his long white beard, and for the first time anyone could remember, he didn't have an answer. The years passed, and Hance became terminally ill. As he lay on his death bed, the last words he uttered were "Where did I put all that dirt?"

Hance's friends remembered him as a man who lived at peace with nature and who loved the wilderness—especially the Grand Canyon.

Our walk to the New Hance trailhead now takes us through a woodland of pinyon pine, several species of juniper, and scattered bushes of cliffrose, fernbush, and mountain mahogany, the latter three members of the rose family. The trees are fully grown, yet hardly reach half-again our height; no wonder such woodlands are often called pygmy forests. The pinyons were especially important to early native people. Of the nine amino acids essential to human growth, seven are present in pinyon nuts. The sweet-tasting nut is a valuable food not only for humans but for birds and mammals including chipmunks, Abert squirrels, and bighorn sheep.

The juniper—the quintessential symbol of the windswept, high plateaus—has an ancient look about it, with its twisted, gnarled trunk, shredding bark, and stunted growth. Indeed, Stanley Welsh, a botanist and director of Monte L. Bean Life Science Museum at Brigham Young University, has counted the tree rings of a Utah juniper, growing on the Kaiparowits Plateau just north of the Grand Canyon, in excess of 1,280 years. He speculates that this particular woodland may be in the range of two thousand years

Above: *Tarantulas searching for a mate are a common sight along the canyon rims in the autumn. (Photo © by H. Knickerbocker.)* **Below**: *South Rim resident, miner, storyteller, and trail guide John Hance entertained tourists visiting the Grand Canyon in the 1880s. (Photo reproduced courtesy of Grand Canyon National Park, Photo #825.)*

Although the beavertail cactus lacks the long spines found on other species of prickly pear cactus, the pads are well-armed with tiny needle-like yellow glochids. (Photo © by H. Knickerbocker.)

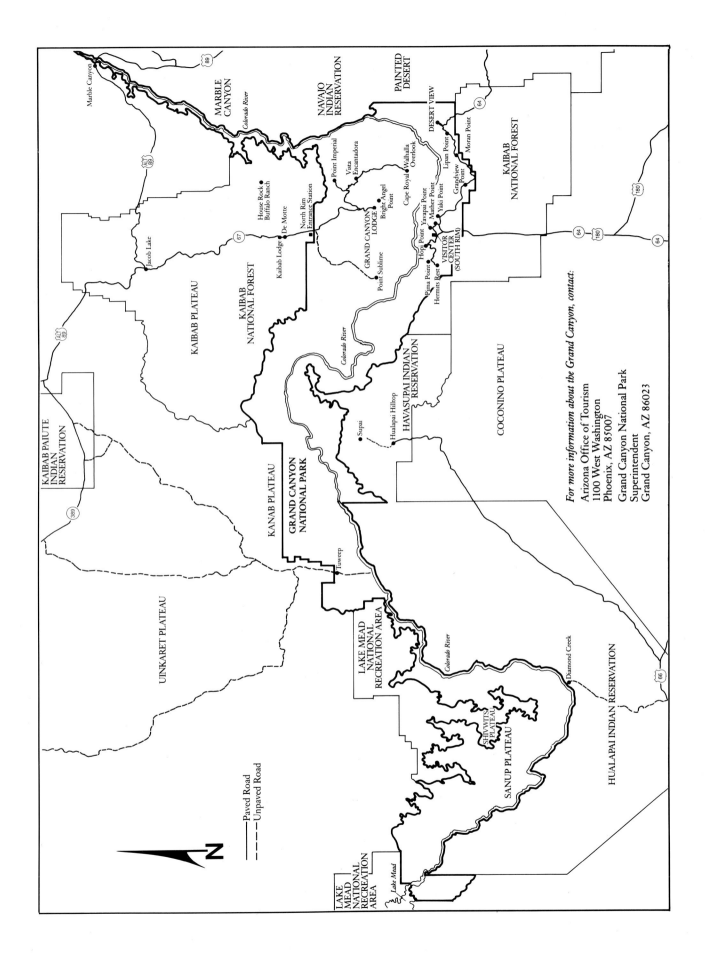

21

old. Most of the South Rim's trees are three hundred to four hundred years old, but a few seem to portray much greater antiquity.

The plants in the woodland around us are well spaced. Limited moisture plays a major role in their distribution, yet there are just enough scraggly branches overhead along with a bristling array of whipple cholla, prickly pear cactus, banana yucca, and sagebrush underfoot to prevent us from traveling in a straight line. As we zig and zag, I keep an eye out for the sentry milk vetch, a rare member of the legume family that is known to grow only in small, shallow pockets and cracks in the limestone.

Beneath our feet the broken chunks of grayish white Kaibab Limestone make walking difficult. It's rather odd that this marine deposit that forms the South Rim stands well over a vertical mile above sea level, nearly seven thousand feet, and hundreds of miles away from the nearest ocean. Yet 250 million years ago a warm shallow sea covered this region. Either the ancient oceans were thousands of feet deeper (not likely) or northern Arizona has undergone dramatic uplifting (the current theory). In this ancient sea, dissolved calcium and carbonate became concentrated to the saturation point and precipitated out as lime mud. The calcium carbonate shells and parts of crinoids (sea lilies), brachiopods, corals, snails, clams, and scaphopods (tusk shells) added to form this lime deposit.

Besides calcium carbonate, the ancient Kaibab sea water contained dissolved silicon dioxide, the same mineral that makes up quartz. When the silicon dioxide precipitated out, nodules of hard, brittle chert were formed. The chert in the Kaibab Limestone layer is usually white or gray, but occasionally iron oxides have colored the chert red (called jasper) or, along this part of the rim, orange.

I lean down and pick up a porcelain-smooth flake of orange-colored chert scattered among the limestone pieces. This hard, glasslike mineral has been fractured into a sharp splinter; little wonder that chert was a favorite arrowhead and tool-making stone. Some three to four thousand years ago, people designated by archaeologists as members of a hunting and gathering culture known as the Pinto Basin Complex passed near this spot and dropped several of their distinctive spear points. Perhaps they, too, were hunting for bighorns.

The Pinto Basin people climbed into caves coursing through the Redwall Limestone deep within the canyon and left behind small animal figurines. These figurines were usually made of willow, cottonwood, or squawbush twigs that had been split lengthwise and twisted and woven into the shape of a deer or bighorn. A deer or bighorn feces pellet might be placed inside the body of the animal. Sometimes the figurine was pierced by a miniature spear. Since the first figurines were discovered in 1933, people have speculated on their use. Perhaps these objects were simply good luck charms, designed to ensure a successful hunt.

Ten figurine cave sites are now known in the Grand Canyon. In addition to the figurines, most of these sites also contain bones or feces from bighorn sheep or Harrington's goat, a relative of the modern mountain goat that became extinct thousands of years before the Pinto people arrived on the scene. In some of the caves the figurines or unworked pieces of twig were placed on or within rock cairns. One recently discovered cave held thirty-three of these "shrines." Paleontologist Steve Emslie suggests that maybe these ancient hunters were not only hoping for a successful bighorn sheep hunt but were also paying homage to its long-extinct relative.

The recent discovery in the western Grand Canyon of the Pinto Basin culture's rock art, which expert Polly Schaafsma describes as "over 40 bizarre, elongated anthropomorphic figures," sheds more mystery than light on these ancient hunters. Archaeologist Douglas Schwartz notes the irony that through the paintings and the figurines we have dramatic glimpses into the hunters' presumably secret, magic rituals, yet we know even less about their everyday lives.

As we continue along the South Rim, we no-

In the warm, shallow Kaibab Sea that covered northern Arizona 250 million years ago flourished crinoids or sea lilies, plantlike animals whose "stems," composed of washer-shaped segments, are sometimes found fossilized in the Kaibab Limestone. (Photo © by Gary Ladd.)

tice an occasional pottery shard lying on the ground. The distinctive black-and-white geometric designs on the broken pieces and plain gray portions of pot rims suggest that the Anasazi, the ancestors of today's Hopi and other Pueblo Native Americans, passed this way, too. The Anasazi lived here much more recently than the Pinto Basin people, only seven hundred to a thousand years ago. Several miles east of here, along the East Rim Drive, are the ruins known today as Tusayan (not to be confused with the community of Tusayan near the south entrance of the park). Between A.D. 1185 and 1200, perhaps thirty Anasazi lived in this U-shaped, stone-walled structure. But this was a time of drought in an already marginal area for farming, and the residents soon abandoned the site.

Also intermingled with the loose stones and shards beneath our feet are signs of modern passage. We see fresh elk and mule deer droppings and an abundance of gray fox and coyote scat.

Seeds in the coyote scat reveal that they have been eating juniper berries, which actually are not berries at all but modified cones. In the canyon area, cottontails and pack rats are the coyote's favorite foods, along with mice, birds, an occasional duck, and a variety of plant material, including grasses, are also consumed. Such a liberal diet has allowed the resourceful coyote to prosper in a wide range of habitats.

The Navajos call the coyote "God's dog." In winter, coyotes might be led to a carcass by listening and then following the raven's call. A flock of feeding ravens usually contains a few members that act as sentinels. If a sentinel gives a warning call because of approaching danger, the coyote will also pay heed. This behavior is exhibited even in newborn coyote pups as they take cover after hearing the raven's warning call for the first time. In the summer as the coyote hunts rodents and rabbits, ravens may follow in the hope of dining on leftover scraps. Just how important this symbiotic relationship is between coyote and raven is not yet fully know, but as the coyote's range has expanded to eastern North America, so has the raven's. And though coyotes may occasionally drive off the ravens, coyotes don't prey upon them.

As we pass by the pinyons and junipers, mountain chickadees and pygmy nuthatches call and glean the tree trunks for tiny insects. Many of the trunks are pockmarked with the drillings of yellow-bellied sapsuckers that passed through during their migrations. In the dry leaves at the base of a Gambel oak, a rufous-sided towhee scratches about, pausing for a moment to emit a catlike call.

Off the rim, we can hear the squawk of a Clark's nutcracker, a typically high alpine resident fairly common in the spruce and fir forest of the North Rim, who may descend to lower elevations during the fall and winter. On rare occasions, the nutcracker nests within pockets of mixed conifers that grow immediately below the South Rim.

A bit of movement near the top of a pinyon pine catches my eye. At first it looks like a grayish brown nest of twigs, but closer examination reveals the little black eyes and soft brown nose of a porcupine hidden in a mass of bristling quills. These slow-moving creatures must rely on their protective quills and coloration to escape predation, although vehicles are a major cause of death today. Foresters abhor the porky's habit of dining on the vital cambial layers of tissue just under a tree's bark. During most of the year, however, porcupines feast on leaves, berries, roots, flowers, seeds, and the parasitic mistletoe. When the menu switches to trees, young saplings are often preferred, which may actually help to thin the forest.

The land now dips slightly into a shallow draw leading to the trailhead. The trail begins in typical Grand Canyon style as a series of steep, knee-wrenching, zig-zagging switchbacks. Here, under the protection of a north-facing cliff, several white fir grow tall and strong, a relict of the last ice age when the canyon climate was cooler and wetter.

24

The much-maligned but adaptable coyote is one of the few animals that has been able to expand its range in North America since the 1800s. (Photo © by Erwin & Peggy Bauer.)

Often seen along the rims and popular trails, variegated rock squirrels become a nuisance when unthinking visitors give them handouts. (Photo © by S. Aitchison.)

A rock squirrel pierces the cool air with a shrill alarm whistle. Along popular trails and view points, the rock squirrels quickly lose their fear of people, especially when they become accustomed to handouts. This unnatural food source usually attracts more and more squirrels until there is an overabundance of them. In some of the more popular camping areas, the park service has erected metal poles from which food can be hung to discourage squirrels from chewing through your backpack at night. This overpopulation also promotes transmission of disease, resulting in potential health problems for both squirrels and humans. Many squirrels may die during the stress of winter, when handouts are more scarce, and from epidemics.

Baby rock squirrels are occasionally preyed upon by snakes. One time on the Kaibab Trail I saw a pair of adult squirrels protecting their nest by attacking a gopher snake. The squirrels took turns approaching the snake from the rear and biting it along its back. Eventually, the snake was mortally wounded and the baby squirrels saved.

We continue down through the three uppermost rock layers of the Grand Canyon—the Kaibab, Toroweap, and Coconino formations—and then scramble across and up to Coronado Butte. This is a good area to see bighorn sheep, and probably early hunters used this lookout, too.

A very approachable herd tends to browse around the Bright Angel trailhead in the Grand Canyon Village. Bighorn become habituated to people in areas where they are not hunted or threatened. The herd here in Red Canyon has not seen many humans, but if they are allowed to get above you, the sheep seem to be more at ease and may spend a considerable amount of time observing you.

From the 1920s, when the park service began to record bighorn sightings, until about twenty years ago, the sheep population seemed to be declining. In 1970 the population was estimated at a mere 150 animals. The decline may have been due to hunting of the sheep prior to the establishment of the park, to disease introduced through domestic livestock, and to range deterioration caused by feral burros.

Since the removal of burros from the park in 1981, bighorn sightings have increased, possibly indicating a corresponding increase in their numbers. In prehistoric times, bighorn apparently ranged throughout the canyon, but today their distribution is patchy. The Arizona Fish and Game Department has recently transplanted bighorns just outside the park boundaries in former historic ranges. Some of these animals or their descendants may eventually enter the park.

From our perch atop Coronado Butte, we can look back at the South Rim. Jutting out from the rim is Grandview Point. I can make out a few people standing at the edge. With just a little imagination, I can almost hear the 1890s stagecoaches from Flagstaff rumbling up to the rim. And there's Captain Hance gesturing toward the abyss, no doubt telling how he wore off the end of his index finger by pointing at the canyon.

My thoughts continue to drift back into history as the sun dips behind the edge of the rim. The angled, warm afternoon light sets the inner canyon aglow, and it's easy to believe that the canyon has always been the same. But nature is never at rest; nor does humankind interact with the world without leaving its imprint.

In the fading light, a magnificent ram steps out onto the ridge between us and the rim. A set of full-curled horns registers many seasons of life. He seems to be surveying his domain, and then silently, he is gone. His ancestors faced the hunter and survived, but today he faces the technocrat and a less certain future.

Bighorn sheep are occasionally encountered early in the morning at the head of the Bright Angel Trail. (Photo © by Stewart Aitchison.)

Pinyon pine, juniper, and yucca are common along the South Rim. (Photo © by Dick Dietrich.)

THE MOUNTAIN
LYING DOWN

The distance from Grand Canyon Village on the South Rim to the Grand Canyon Lodge on the Kaibab Plateau portion of the North Rim is eleven miles as the raven flies, about twice that distance by trail, and over two hundred miles by road. During the winter, when the North Rim roads are snowed in, the Kaibab Plateau seems especially remote and mysterious. From our perch here on the canyon's south side, my friend Jim and I have planned a cross-country ski trip to penetrate that wintery plateau.

To reach the North Rim, we leave the park via the Desert View Entrance Station and drop down onto the Navajo Indian Reservation. The drive takes us across several hours of high desert, through a corner of the Painted Desert—a land of nitrogen-poor, barren claystones and mudstones splashed with sun-blasted shades of pastel—and on through blackbrush and big sage flats spread along the sandy base of the hogback known as the Echo Cliffs.

From about the Tuba City turnoff to Lee's Ferry and then west along the base of the Vermilion Cliffs, Highway 89 parallels the historic Honeymoon Trail, the route taken during the 1870s and 1880s by many northern Arizona Mormon newlyweds after having their civil union sanctified at the Saint George Temple in Utah. Their campsites are marked now by green oases of Fremont cottonwoods and Lombardy poplars that they planted at seeps and springs

along the cliffs to provide shady relief from the desert sun.

The highway skirts the heads of Salt Water Wash and Jackass Canyon, major tributaries leading to the Colorado River, before turning west to cross Marble Canyon, the very beginning of the Grand Canyon. We cross the Navajo Bridge and leave the Navajo Nation. The graceful span was built in 1928 to replace the treacherous river crossing at Lee's Ferry a few miles upstream. A new bridge designed for today's larger and faster vehicles is currently being constructed parallel to the original.

We are now on the north side of the Colorado River and have entered the Arizona Strip, a large swath of desolate country politically tied to Arizona but geographically, culturally, and economically linked to southern Utah.

The highway curves along the base of the soaring Vermilion Cliffs. To the south and west the land appears at first flat, but shallow undulations hide huge tributary canyons emptying into Marble Canyon.

A flash of horn larks soar over the road, and a sign announces House Rock Valley Buffalo Ranch off to the south. We turn onto the dirt track and head toward Saddle Mountain, which overlooks the Nankoweap area of the Grand Canyon.

A small herd of pronghorn race across our road, but no sign of the buffalo. Buffalo, more

31

Skiing across a sinkhole on the North Rim. (Photo © by Stewart Aitchison.)

correctly called bison, didn't occur in Arizona in historic times. By 1886, after millions of these great animals were mindlessly slaughtered, less than six hundred of the woolly beasts were left in the lower forty-eight states. Extinction seemed certain; however, one ex-buffalo hunter, Charles Jesse "Buffalo" Jones, began roping bison calves in the hopes of breeding them and perpetuating the species. Jones also had a scheme to interbreed bison with cattle to produce hybrid animals that displayed the virtues of both parents—long, silky hair, delicious meat, a capacity to eat tough, scrubby range plants, and an ability to cope with a harsh climate.

In 1906, Jones was granted permission by the federal government to conduct his breeding experiments within the Grand Canyon Forest Reserve—later to become the national park and adjacent national forest—on the Kaibab Plateau. Unforeseen problems arose. Foremost was the fact that the bison preferred the more open country of House Rock Valley. The herd soon left the Kaibab Forest and headed down to the desert scrublands of the Marble Platform.

Jones faced other problems as well. While the domestic heifers would readily breed with bison bulls, they produced male calves that were sterile; the calves' thick coats kept the reproductive organs at too high a temperature. The persistence of the bison's hump in the fetus also made delivery difficult or even impossible without human assistance. The first "cattalo" experiments were deemed a financial failure.

Jones eventually sold out to James "Uncle Jim" Owens, who maintained the herd until 1927 when they were purchased by the state of Arizona. Today a couple of hundred bison roam among wild herds of pronghorn in the shadow of the Saddle Mountain Wilderness Area.

As we near the mountain, more and more snow covers the road until, just short of the designated wilderness, a huge drift blocks further progress. Much of the North Rim is over eight

thousand feet above sea level and receives over two hundred inches of snow each winter. The paved forty-five-mile road from Jacob Lake to the North Rim lodge is usually closed to vehicles from November to May, but it has become *de rigueur* to cross-country ski the snow-packed road across the Kaibab Plateau to the North Rim. Jim and I are scouting out a shorter route. On the topo map, it appears that a course might exist from near the head of Saddle Canyon, along a ridge to the high Kaibab Plateau, skirting around the rim of Nankoweap, to a breathtaking overlook at Point Imperial.

Skis are clipped on, bulging packs hefted, and off we go huffing and puffing up the ridge, but the snow could be deeper. With every few kick-and-glides there is a distressing crunch of ski bottom against rock. We tie our skis to our backpacks and continue climbing on foot.

As we cross a sparse stand of leafless New Mexican locust, I notice a patch of snow that looks like a pile of mashed potatoes. Something

has stirred the snowpack. A closer look first reveals numerous mule deer tracks, then spots of blood and torn pieces of deer hide. And there, only slightly melted out, are a set of mountain lion tracks. I'm glad to see that at least one lion still exists on the North Rim.

From the 1890s to 1930, the Kaibab Plateau was the scene for a classic study in range and wildlife mismanagement. To the early Anglo-explorers, the area was known as Buckskin Mountain in reference to the herds of mule deer that summered in the Kaibab's woods and flower-carpeted meadows. As the land came under the jurisdiction of the federal government, land managers felt that these deer herds and other "good" animals should be enhanced. A program to eliminate predators was thus initiated. As expressed by no less than Teddy Roosevelt, "Important . . . work is to keep down the larger beasts and birds of prey, the archenemies of the deer, mountain sheep, and grouse." Buffalo Jones summed up the general attitude of the time: It is our duty "to subdue and utilize nature."

Between 1906 and 1924, an estimated 3,024 coyotes, 674 mountain lions, and twenty-one wolves were removed from the Kaibab area, primarily by shooting and trapping. One of the government hunters was Uncle Jim Owens. On the trail to his cabin, a sign proclaimed, "Lions caught to order, Reasonable Rates." His cabin walls were studded with hundreds of lion claws giving mute testimony to his hunting prowess. Besides traps and guns, another rather unique method was employed to remove lions.

It started when, in 1908, a struggling author by the name of Zane Grey visited the West to gain firsthand experience of the frontier. He, Buffalo Jones, and James Emett, a ferryman at Lee's Ferry, rode out to the remote Powell Plateau that juts out into the canyon as a forest-shrouded peninsula. They planned to lasso lions and ship them to zoos back east.

By using hounds, the men succeeded in first treeing a lion and then precariously tossing several loops of rope over the beast's head. With feet tied together, several fiesty, snarling lions were packed out of the canyon on the backs of nervous horses.

At the same time that these natural predators were being destroyed or removed, livestock numbers on the Kaibab were being reduced. By the turn of the century, the Kaibab Plateau had been so badly overgrazed by hundreds of thousands of sheep, tens of thousands of cattle, and unknown numbers of horses and dairy cows, that ranchers began to move their animals elsewhere.

With the elimination of predators and reduced competition with livestock, the stage was set for the Kaibab deer herd population to grow. And grow it did. From a low of about four thousand mule deer in 1906, the herds soon escalated to more than one hundred thousand animals. During the winter of 1924–25, this misguided management came to a disastrous head. The carrying capacity of the range had been grossly exceeded. An estimated 75 percent of the previous year's fawns died during the winter. Thousands of deer

Mt. Hayden pierces the clouds. View from Point Imperial, North Rim. (Photo © by Dick Dietrich.)

continued to die in the succeeding years. Both the folly of predator control and the need to supervise livestock grazing became increasingly apparent.

Several attempts were made to remove the excess deer to other areas. One idea, attributed to Zane Grey, was to herd deer down the Nankoweap Trail, swim them across the Colorado River, and come out the Tanner Trail to the South Rim. One hundred twenty-five men were to deliver no less than three thousand and no more than eight thousand deer.

Armed with tin cans and cowbells, the men formed a line. With a crash, the line moved forward, men hollering and clanging their noisemakers. With each stop, the line wavered and became more disorganized. A threatening storm became a reality. By the time the line reached the head of the Nankoweap Trail, "There were no deer in front of the men but thousands of deer behind them." (Russo 1964)

The Kaibab Plateau still supports large herds of deer, as anyone who has driven through the large meadows at dusk can testify, but gone is the wolf and virtually every mountain lion. Ironically, mule deer herds have declined dramatically in other parts of the Arizona Strip. The Bureau of Land Management believes that suitable deer habitat has declined because of the removal of domestic sheep, emphasis on managing the range for cattle, and aggressive fire suppression. These three factors have decreased both the succulent forage on summer ranges and the young nutritious browse on winter ranges necessary to sustain the deer population. Managing land for the benefit of both livestock and wildlife is a tricky balancing act.

After a couple of hours of climbing, we have ascended nearly a thousand vertical feet; the snowpack is getting thicker, and the plateau seems to be within reach. The ridge flattens out for a few hundred yards and we decide to put our skis back on. This is great! A couple more hours and we should be on top of the world!

Kick, glide, kick, glide, and then, suddenly, our ridge abruptly ends. A hundred-foot-deep notch is cut into the ridge. There's no way down and across and no way around. Our only recourse is to go back down to the car. *All the way back down.*

We collapse in disappointment, but as we sit there, the incredible scene around us begins to soak in. Without the pressure of an objective pushing us on, we can take the time to appreciate the beauty that is right before us.

Looking back toward the north across the Marble Platform to the Vermilion Cliffs, I can see a string of lenticular clouds, a promise of an approaching storm. I think of other travelers to this rugged country. In the fateful year of 1776, Fathers Silvestre Vélez de Escalante and Francisco Atanasio Domìnguez were searching for an overland route from Santa Fe, New Mexico, to the missions at Monterey, California. Early winter storms in the Great Basin country of western Utah forced the expedition to retreat. Instead of retracing their steps, the men chose a more southerly course which took them across the Arizona Strip country. They attempted but failed to cross the Colorado River where the infamous Mormon John D. Lee would locate his ferry nearly one hundred years later. The padres eventually found a route over the Echo Cliffs, forded the river upstream in Glen Canyon, and made their way back to Santa Fe.

On the west side of the Marble Platform the land rises like a monstrous wave. This flexure in the earth's crust is known to geologists as the Kaibab Monocline, which trends north-south some one hundred miles. The highway climbs the back of this wave in a series of looping switchbacks, up and up, leaving the desert scrub behind. First junipers and then pinyons appear, soon followed by ponderosa pine. By the time you reach Jacob Lake, you have gained nearly three thousand feet in elevation from the Marble Platform. Though high and in places rolling, the Kaibab Plateau lacks defined peaks or summits, which led the Paiute to call this place "the mountain lying down," or Kaibab.

Instead of retreating to the car, Jim and I decide that since we have expended all this effort to reach this panoramic location we will camp

Golden aspens and spruce, De Motte Park, Kaibab National Forest. (Photo © by Gary Ladd.)

Above: *In 1908, Zane Grey teamed up with Buffalo Jones and Jim Emmett to lasso mountain lions on the Powell Plateau and send them to zoos. The idea was to remove predators to encourage the growth of the Kaibab deer herd. (Photo reproduced courtesy of Zane Grey, Inc.)*
Below: *Author Zane Grey spent many days exploring the Grand Canyon and used the canyon as a backdrop for several of his western novels. (Photo reproduced courtesy of Zane Grey, Inc.)*

The graceful span of Navajo Bridge across Marble Canyon was completed in 1928 and eliminated the need of crossing the Colorado River by ferry, a crossing that sometimes ended in tragedy. (Photo © by S. Aitchison.)

here overnight. In the fading light, we brew some tea over a little stove and drink in the scene before us.

I muse over a trip I took on the strip one time in late summer. Ann and I had just gassed up at Jacob Lake, and rather than turning south to go to the Grand Canyon Lodge at the North Rim, we decided to follow one of the gravel forest service roads that lead off the northwest side of the Kaibab down toward Kanab Canyon, the largest tributary canyon coming into the Grand Canyon from the north. Piles of pine slash and freshly sawn stumps gave testimony to the intensive logging taking place on the national forest. "Scenic corridors" of virgin timber along the paved tourist road to the North Rim concealed the work of the timber industry.

We saw no evidence that day of the unique Kaibab squirrel, an endemic subspecies of the tassel-eared squirrel, that lives in the ponderosa pine forest. Biologists believe that prior to the carving of the Grand Canyon the Abert's squirrel of the South Rim and the Kaibab squirrel of the North Rim were the same species. Millions of years of isolation have allowed the North Rim population to evolve into a different subspecies.

Both types of squirrels feed primarily on ponderosa pine during part of the year. After studying the Kaibab squirrel for decades, zoologist Joseph Hall has concluded that any negative impact the squirrel may have on the pine is insignificant compared to the accompanying benefits. By feeding on the trees, the squirrels spread the spores of certain hypogenous (subterranean) fungi and bolete mushrooms that aid the tree's root hairs in absorbing minerals. In turn, the fungi receive some of their nourishment from the carbon produced by the tree's photosynthesis. Nature has engineered a nice three-way arrangement that benefits squirrel, pine, and fungus.

Kaibab squirrels are closely linked to the ponderosa pine for nesting sites as well as for food. They tend to nest in clumps of pine where the tree crowns interlock. The trees are typically fif-

Mountain lions, or cougars, were nearly exterminated from the Grand Canyon in the early part of this century because of the mistaken belief that predator control would benefit deer. The deer population on the North Rim exploded, resulting in extreme overgrazing and browsing of the natural vegetation and, eventually, many deer dying of starvation. Today the lion population seems to be making a slow recovery, and the deer herd sizes are closer to the natural carrying capacity of the land. (Photo © by S. Aitchison.)

Overleaf: *The South Rim may receive close to one hundred inches of snow each winter. The higher North Rim can get twice that amount. (Photo © by Les Manevitz.)*

As ponderosa pines mature, their bark changes color from dark gray or black to a wonderful golden brown. (Photo © by Les Manevitz.)

Above: *The Abert squirrel is ecologically tied to the ponderosa pine forest found along the South Rim. In the North Rim pine forest lives the Kaibab squirrel. Biologists believe that the Abert and Kaibab squirrels had a common ancestor, but as the Southwest became drier and hotter and forests retreated to higher elevations, the two populations of squirrels have become isolated from each other. Enough time has passed for evolution to create squirrels with slightly differently colored fur coats.* **Below**: *A Kaibab squirrel. (Both photos © by Tom & Pat Leeson.)*

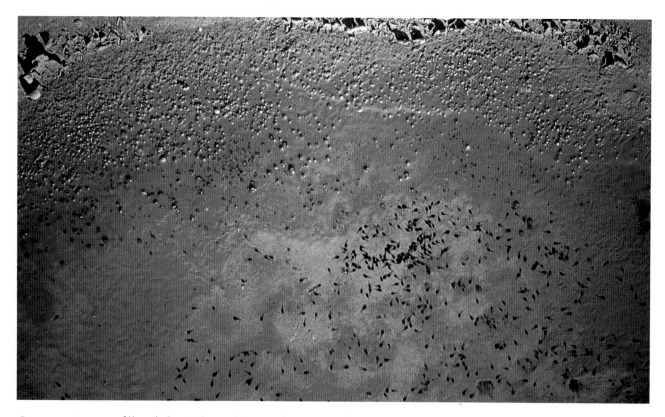

Summer rainstorms fill potholes in the sandstone with water. A few days of warm sunshine can lead to an amazing hatching of tadpoles, fairy shrimp, and aquatic insects. (Photo © by Steve Mulligan.)

teen to twenty inches in diameter and over one hundred years old. As the older pines are logged and the forest "opened up," the squirrels have fewer choices for nesting. The pine forest within the park boundaries, where logging is prohibited, may become their only refuge.

To further ensure the Kaibab squirrel's survival, the Arizona Game and Fish Department has transplanted squirrels to the ponderosa pine forests of the Uinkaret Mountains, a volcanic range west of Toroweap Valley and immediately north of the Grand Canyon.

My first visit to the Toroweap Valley and Uinkaret Mountains was in 1965, when this section of the Grand Canyon was still designated a national monument. The monument was incorporated into the national park in 1975. I remember stopping at the Tuweep Ranger Station for directions:

Ranger John Riffey passed another plate of homemade chocolate chip cookies. As I munched away, I didn't realize at the time that I was snacking with one of the canyon's legendary figures. Since 1942, Riffey had been the one-man staff of Grand Canyon National Monument. He acted as superintendent, ranger, naturalist, and interpreter. On foot, truck, horseback, and in his airplane—appropriately nicknamed Pegasus—Riffey patrolled over three hundred square miles of forest, desert, canyon, and mountain. Although he cherished his solitude in Toroweap Valley, he enjoyed the company of the infrequent tourists that ventured to his part of the Grand Canyon.

A few miles down from his "front yard," we arrived at the Toroweap Overlook—not a good place to be if you suffer from acrophobia. Just thinking about the nearly vertical three-thousand-foot drop to the Colorado River makes my knees weak and my heart pound. Be forewarned that some sadistic canyon sage will invariably tell you about the tourist who, after snapping a few shots, turned around to walk away but lost his balance and fell backward into the abyss, with eyes bugged out and only shocked silence escaping a gaping mouth.

Our night in the campground at the rim was shattered by a tremendous lightning storm. The thunder woke us up. We watched the amazing light show approach from the southwest, cross Prospect Canyon, and beat down on Lava Falls Rapid far below before slamming into us. Bits of static electricity jumped and popped about like popcorn. We retreated to the relative safety of our car.

In the morning light, we could see that dozens of potholes in the sandstone were now brimming with rainwater. The warm sun would cause a remarkable hatching to take place in these ephemeral pools. Within hours algae, bacteria, and protozoans would appear. In a day or two fairy shrimp, clam shrimp, and tadpole shrimp would hatch. A species of mosquito and one of gnat that breed only in temporary water pockets might also appear, along with toads, snails, spiders, and dragonflies. The amount and diversity of life that springs from the desert dust after a rain is simply amazing. If all goes well, the creatures procreate before the water completely evaporates. Some of the adult animals, like the snail and toad, burrow in for a long wait. The shrimp eggs become entombed in the drying mud, but the adults die and their fragile bodies crumble and blow away.

We waited until late afternoon before leaving to give the dirt road over to the ghost town of Mount Trumbull a chance to dry out. The still-slippery road gave us a few nervous moments as we dropped a thousand feet off the great fault escarpment of the Hurricane Cliffs. We were entering the loneliest, least accessible portion of the Arizona Strip, the Shivwits Plateau.

Not far west of the Hurricane Cliffs, we passed through the crumbling ruins of Mount Trumbull, sometimes called Bundyville. During the 1920s and 1930s as many as fifteen hundred people attempted to farm this area—a losing proposition in this arid valley. Our ultimate goal was to cross the Shivwits Plateau and reach the Grand Wash Cliffs, which mark not only the western edge of the plateau but the end of the Grand Canyon.

Out here there are few signs and even fewer people, but we kept consulting the topo maps and heading west. As we traversed this desolate land, I pondered the mysterious fate of three who chose this path so many years ago.

Late in the summer of 1869, fearing that the raging rapids of the Colorado River would kill them all, three of Major John Wesley Powell's brave men left his river expedition. The Howland brothers, Oramel and Seneca, and Bill Dunn hiked out Separation Canyon to the rim of the Shivwits Plateau and were never seen again. Several years later, Powell engaged Mormon missionary and pathfinder Jacob Hamblin to help him solve the mystery. During their exploration of the plateau, Powell and Hamblin encountered a band of Shivwits Paiutes. With Hamblin translating, the Indians confessed to murdering the hapless trio. The Shivwits explained that they had mistaken the three men for a group of prospectors who had raped a Shivwits woman.

But was this the true story? Was Hamblin translating correctly or merely fabricating a story? Recent revelations point to possible Mormon involvement in the men's demise. Flagstaff writer and mystery sleuth Scott Thybony reports, "An old document that has recently surfaced mentions the murder of three men, not in the remote Shivwits country, but in the Mormon town of Toquerville." Could these have been Powell's men? If so, what was the motive for the murder? Will the canyon someday yield the answers?

A cold wind brings me back to the snowy ridge. Jim is already snoring. A light snow is falling. I snuggle deeper into my down cocoon and wondered what other secrets the canyon country holds. As a Havasupai man told Father Escalante two centuries ago, this land has been formed by the Rio Grande de los Misterios, "The Great River of Mystery." Maybe tomorrow we will find a route to the rim. Maybe tomorrow we will stumble across an answer to a canyon mystery.

Overleaf: *Lightning from Point Sublime on North Rim. (Photo © by Dick Dietrich.)*

View from near Yaki Point, South Rim. (Photo © by Dick Dietrich.)

THE RAVEN'S VIEW

Almost without fail, walking a short distance east of Yaki Point will bring me the company of a shiny, jet black raven. The bird lands in a dead juniper or on the ground and cocks its head toward me, no doubt expecting a delectable treat. I approach closer and the raven jumps back. When no food is forthcoming, the bird leaps off into space, gives a *kukuk* chase call, and joins its friends cartwheeling, dogfighting, and tumbling out over the Grand Canyon.

Sometimes in the deep quietness of a side-canyon, a raven's wing will *swish, swish* overhead. At other times, the bird's flight is silent like an owl's. One ornithologist suggests that the noise occurs when ravens fly in difficult, windy conditions, but I have usually heard it on dead-calm days. Roland Case Ross, writing in a 1925 issue of *Condor,* thought "this was a volitional effort, as numbers of times a pair of birds would go overhead and only one would be giving the sound." Ross wondered if the activity could be sexual in nature, perhaps a subtle way to identify one's self or to impress one's mate.

Ravens enjoy a unique perspective of the Grand Canyon. They soar overhead, dive to the bottom, hop around on tiny rock ledges, explore side-canyons large and small. Their indiscriminate taste allows them to dine on a wide array of foods, from carrion to insects. They rarely drink. Their shiny bluish black feathers absorb the sun's radiant energy, protecting the body within from overheating. All of these characteristics are important to the raven's survival in the arid climate of the Grand Canyon.

One early spring, two other biologists and I were camped out on the Tonto Platform above and just west of Phantom Ranch, the tourist lodge located in the inner canyon where Bright Angel Creek meets the Colorado River. We were there, primarily, to collect (the field biologist's euphemism for "trap and stuff") small mammals for continuing taxonomic and geographic distribution studies done by the Museum of Northern Arizona and National Park Service, but an early morning bird census seemed like a good idea, too.

As the first rays of sunlight lit up Zoroaster Temple, we slid out of sleeping bags, grabbed binoculars and a granola bar, and ambled through the scrubby blackbrush. Halfway through the musical descending notes of a canyon wren, a Cessna barely cleared Cheops Pyramid, its engine roar echoing off the Redwall cliffs. The plane banked steeply over Bright Angel Canyon—no doubt to get a better view of Phantom Ranch—then turned to the west, apparently to follow the Colorado River.

Before the noise completely abated, a larger, two-engine craft droned overhead, then the *whomp, whomp, whomp* and whine of a turbojet helicopter shattered the quiet. High in the troposphere, contrails of commercial jetliners began

Ravens are ubiquitous sentinels of the Grand Canyon. Their catholic diet helps to ensure their survival in this harsh environment. (Photo © by S. Aitchison.)

to interweave and jet engine rumbles roiled down upon the landscape. One gas hawk after another essentially blotted out any bird song there might have been. Even the loud call of the raven couldn't compete. We recorded thirty-seven overflights in less than an hour.

That spring morning was in 1973. By 1986, the National Park Service was reporting as many as 274 flights per day. An outcry of concern arose from the conservation community urging the park service to do something about the airplane noise problem. The park service, however, had no legal jurisdiction over the air traffic. Eventually, Congress was enjoined to force the Federal Aviation Administration to take action.

While the FAA was considering its options, more issues were being raised. Air tour operators claimed that their flights had no impact on the canyon, but simply enabled people to see more remote areas. The conservationists claimed that the noise ruined the wilderness experience of back-country users and that motor vibration knocked endangered peregrine falcon eggs off ledges and rattled Indian ruins apart; they called for a "level of natural quiet" to be determined for the Grand Canyon as had been done for Canyonlands National Park in Utah. Biologists could only speculate on the ecological consequences of overflights since no research had been done in the canyon.

Some friends and I experienced another type of flight impact one day while we were ascending a climber's route out of the Little Colorado River Gorge. A jet broke the sound barrier above us, and the resulting shock wave released a small avalanche of rocks that sent us scurrying for cover.

The controversy raged on, but there was little national publicity about the canyon's air traffic and noise pollution—until one spring day in 1986. Tour planes and helicopters were out as usual. At Crystal Rapid, a rafting party looked up in horror as a helicopter and plane collided.

Both craft dropped like stones; all twenty-five people aboard perished. The issue shifted from noise pollution to air safety.

While the debate continued, studies were being conducted to confirm some of the environmental impacts being claimed. A biological study by Craig Stockwell and Gary Bateman regarding the impact of aircraft on bighorn sheep indicated that sheep are less efficient at foraging when aircraft approach closely. The animal's heart rate increases, and the sheep tend to walk around more, especially during the winter. The biologists speculate that these factors could reduce the fitness of the adults, thereby affecting their reproductive success. Other researchers have noted that lambs become agitated and stumble more often when aircraft are near—a problem which could have disastrous consequences considering where these creatures roam.

Special Federal Aviation Regulations were finally implemented in 1988 and 1989. Flight-free zones were established around the Desert View, Bright Angel, Shinumo, and the Toroweap/ Thunder River areas. Minimum flight altitudes, minimum terrain clearance, and other regulations cover the remaining canyon areas. Congress mandated a thorough study of aircraft sound impacts to be completed before termination of these regulations on June 15, 1992. The FAA will then decide whether or not to continue or to modify these rules.

The raven returns, drifting effortlessly over the canyon. A dark shadow races across the sun-drenched cliffs and terraces.

Although the Grand Canyon can still appear breathtakingly bright and crystal clear—especially following a cold front—today's visitor may unfortunately witness an entirely different scene. Air pollution in the form of fine particulates, primarily sulfates, from urban and industrial sources often clouds the view. The Environmental Protection Agency predicts that these emissions will double in the West between 1985 and 2010. Current legislation will even permit such an increase, following the partial repeal of the 1977 Clean Air Act amendments designed to protect national parks and wilderness areas from visibility degradation.

Much of the pollution in the canyon today is

Air pollution is an increasing problem in the Grand Canyon. The Environmental Protection Agency plans to propose strict and expensive pollution controls on the nearby coal-fired Navajo Generating Station. The operators of the power plant argue that the haze is caused by a variety of sources. (Photo © by Dick Dietrich.)

an ironic consequence of a victory won for the environment in the past. During the 1960s, conservationists succeeded in preventing the construction of two hydroelectric dams—one near Redwall Cavern and the other at Bridge Canyon—that would have backed water into reservoirs. These two dams had been planned to generate electricity to pump Colorado River water to the planned Central Arizona Project (CAP), a scheme to bring water to the Phoenix and Tucson areas.

With the dam issue dead, the CAP had to find other sources of power. The solution was to help fund the construction of the giant 2,250-megawatt Navajo Generating Station about eighty miles northeast of the center of the Grand Canyon. The power plant would burn coal strip-mined from sacred Hopi and Navajo lands atop Black Mesa.

According to the National Park Service's Winter Haze Intensive Tracer Experiment done in 1987, the power plant accounts for 40 to 70 percent of the sulfate pollution in the canyon during the winter. The plant burns more than twenty-four thousand tons of coal per day, releasing twelve to thirteen tons of sulfur dioxide gas into the air hourly. The sulfur dioxide gas eventually transforms into fine particles of ammonium sulfate, which impairs visibility. These findings make the Navajo Generating Station the largest *single* source of sulfur emissions in the entire West.

Additionally, the U.S. Fish and Wildlife Service claims that striped bass caught in Lake Powell near the power plant contain three times as much selenium, a toxic mineral, as fish caught 140 miles upstream. Large-mouth bass, walleye, and crappie also were found to have high levels of selenium, apparently derived from the burning of coal in the power plant. Selenium is concentrated as it moves through the food chain.

Ironically, another federal agency, the Bureau of Reclamation, owns 24.3 percent of the power station and disputes the park service's sulphur dioxide findings. Polly Hays, a physical scientist with the National Park Service, considers the problem to have "progressed out of the realm of science to a political issue." The Environmental Protection Agency has the authority to act, but courts have given the owners of the power plant a time extension to do their own study. Public hearings will then be held to debate the EPA's proposal.

On this spring day, the air is exceptionally clear. Yet I have been here on a winter day when the air smelled foul and the buttes and temples only halfway across the canyon were obscured by the haze. There is no question that the power plant belches out tons of noxious wastes. There is no question that the original agreements between the power companies and the government state that, as technology becomes available, pollution control devices could be installed. There is no question that the Grand Canyon and surrounding Colorado Plateau region once had one of the cleanest airsheds in the nation. Does it really matter whether the pollution goes into the Grand Canyon or Glen Canyon National Recreation Area or out across the Navajo Reservation? Shouldn't every effort be made to stop the fouling of our air? Operators of the plant argue that the cost will be enormous. The park service estimates a $500 million to $1 billion price tag; the Salt River Project, the operators of the plant, suggest $1.6 billion, and the EPA believes the final bill may be $4 billion. Expensive, indeed, but what are the costs of *not* having clean air?

The raven returns again, just to be sure that I haven't dropped a tasty morsel on the ground. This largest of the world's songbirds, intelligent and adaptable, manages to survive in some of nature's most demanding habitats, from the arctic to the tropics. But if we continue to foul our own nest, can even the raven survive? Will we heed the warning to pollute nevermore?

Helicopter and other aircraft noise has been a problem in the Grand Canyon. New regulations are an attempt to mitigate noise pollution. (Photo © by S. Aitchison.)

Silver Grotto in Shinumo Wash, a tributary to Marble Canyon. (Photo © by Dan Polin.)

THE COLORADO RIVER

The time had finally come to row my own raft through the entire Grand Canyon. My boat was small, as Colorado River boats go, only sixteen feet long. My three passengers were enjoying lunch, but I couldn't eat. My stomach was tied in knots. I kept pacing the shore, looking at "The Hole," a depression in the river's surface immediately downstream of a slightly submerged rock. Some holes can actually be fun to run, but in the case of Crystal Rapid at this particular water stage, this hole could easily swallow a whale.

Scott, the trip leader, kept reassuring me in a calm, experienced voice. "Don't worry about the hole. Just keep away from the rocks near the right bank. There's so much water skirting the hole, there's no way you'll get that far left. Keep your stern pointed slightly left and upstream so you can pull away from those rocks."

"Okay, okay," I replied, knowing full well I was about to die.

Lunch was finally over. The passengers were geared up for an exciting ride. I ran down behind a nearby tamarisk for a bit of privacy; fear has a strange way of activating the bladder. I double-checked the line securing the waterproof river bags to the rowing frame. I double-knotted my life jacket, carefully coiled the bowline, and took my seat. I wiped my sweaty hands on my shorts and put a death grip on the oars.

Here, in the calm eddy above the rapid, one could almost forget what lay downstream. And then a low, reverberating roar filled my ears. I felt sick.

I rowed out a short distance, and the downstream current caught me. I stood up for a better view. The smooth green river seemed to drop off the edge of the world; only the occasional splash of whitewater betrayed what was ahead. Now I could see a smooth hump in the water just left of center—the submerged rock that forms the hole. I saw the rock garden along the right bank, my real concern.

I sat down and turned the raft so the bow was slightly to the right. The river's current carried me downstream. A cushion of water off the submerged rock was pushing me right, so with this ferry angle, I would be ready to pull away from the rocky right side.

The raft began to pick up speed. I started to row, slowly at first. Those rocks seemed to be farther out in the river than I remembered. I rowed harder. Geez, those rocks were coming up pretty fast. I rowed harder. The adrenaline was beginning to kick in. I really cranked on the oars.

Then I noticed something out of the corner of my eye. Oh, shit! I had pulled so hard left that I was heading broadside for the hole. Too late to miss it, I pulled with the left oar while push-

Negotiating the rapids of the Colorado River within the Grand Canyon has become a very popular activity. Mitigating the impact caused by the twenty thousand or so annual boaters is a continuing challenge to the National Park Service. (Photo © by Ron Sanford.)

ing with the right. The raft pivoted so the bow was facing the hole just as we went over the hump.

Time seemed to shift into slow motion. Balanced for an instant, I saw a bottomless pit before me, its far wall rising in a huge, backcurling wave. I screamed, "Hang on!" and into the abyss we dropped. The wave crashed down on top of us in a fury; for a long moment all was dark and quiet. *Where am I?* But then I saw light, beautiful blue sky dappled with puffy white clouds. I finally realized that I was lying in the bottom of the boat still gripping the oars. I sat up and yelled, "We made it! We made it!" But no one was there to hear.

My three passengers were gone. I looked around and saw Margaret hanging onto the side of the raft. I reached over to help her into the front compartment, but when I let go, she disappeared. My God, the rubber floor must be gone! She popped up alongside and I helped her in again. This time, though, she straddled the thwart tube.

We spotted Bob clinging to a boulder in the middle of the river. He let go and drifted down to a waiting boat. But where was Ann?

This was Ann's first river trip. She had just hiked down to Phantom Ranch that morning and joined us. Her first day on the river and I had lost her.

By this time, we had somehow ricocheted through the rest of the rapid and I pulled over to the beach. All eyes scanned the river for the body, but to no avail. "I've killed her," I sobbed.

Suddenly, we spotted her *walking* down the beach. She was alive—and not only alive, but unscathed.

In a shaky voice she explained, "It was very dark down there. I thought I was going to die, and there was absolutely nothing I could do about it. Then suddenly, the river spit me out. I was right next to shore, so I just stood up and walked down here."

Thankfully, everyone was fine, but the river had exacted a toll. The front half of the raft floor was peeled back like a banana. The crashing wave had apparently pushed the unlucky threesome down through the floor. The commissary, cast-iron Dutch ovens, griddles, and assorted pots and pans—all of which had been so carefully lashed to the frame—were gone. And the nylon rain jacket Ann had been wearing under her life preserver had been stripped away.

Crystal Rapid did not exist until December of 1966, when fourteen inches of rain fell in thirty-six hours on the heavy snowpack of the North Rim. A tremendous forty-foot wall of flood-water came down Crystal Canyon rolling and pushing car-size boulders into the river. The Colorado rearranged the rocks but couldn't remove the larger ones. Although the Colorado's flow is usually much greater than any flood down a tributary canyon, the side-stream's gradient is steeper, creating more mechanical power than the flatter river.

Such raw power makes an impression upon a novice river runner. So *this* is the tamed Colorado River, whose reckless flow has been harnessed by a series of dams! I shudder to think about the predam floods.

The untamed river was first successfully descended by Major John Wesley Powell in 1869. The best maps of the mid-nineteenth century labeled the vast canyon area of southern Utah and northern Arizona as "unexplored." Undaunted by the loss of his right arm at the Battle of Shiloh, Powell, a self-taught geologist, felt that a daring exploration of this unknown region would lead to congressional support of further geographic and geologic studies. His completed river journey signaled the inception of the systematic study and survey of the Colorado Plateau.

Powell's continued study of the Colorado Plateau and its river resources led him to conclude: "There is not enough water to irrigate all these lands; there is not sufficient water to irrigate all the lands which could be irrigated, and only a small portion can be irrigated. . . . I tell you, gentlemen, you are piling up a heritage of conflict . . . for there is not sufficient water to supply the land."

Unfortunately, Powell's ideas fell upon deaf congressional ears. Despite these early warnings, politicians have encouraged water reclamation projects and land-use schemes that are often impractical, if not impossible, in the arid Southwest.

The fledgling Bureau of Reclamation under the direction of Arthur Powell Davis, nephew of the great explorer, envisioned a series of dams to provide water for crops, power for cities, and a tourist economy for the desert Southwest. This plan became known as the Colorado River Storage Project. Reclamation projects of such a magnitude were impossible to finance for irrigation alone, but became economically justified when the production of electric power could be sold at a profit. Thus the stage was set for construction of the world's largest artificial reservoirs behind hydroelectric dams.

This river of silty water "too thick to drink yet too thin to plow" was seen as a menace to be tamed by building a series of dams. The prehistoric Anasazi had farmed the sandy shoreline and diverted water from side-streams, but their simple technology had little impact on the flow of the main river. Not until the concrete and rebar culture arrived on the scene was the river in any real danger of being subdued.

The first dam authorized was Boulder Dam in 1928, now called Hoover Dam, about forty-five miles west of the canyon. Seven years later, it was completed. The resulting Lake Mead backs up about thirty miles into the Grand Canyon when full, at which point the lake holds two years' worth of the Colorado's flow. The backing up of Lake Mead beyond the Grand Wash Cliffs into the Grand Canyon, beyond the mouths of Quartermaster, Burnt, Horseflat, Surprise, Spencer, and Separation had one immediate, obvious impact on the canyon: The slack waters drowned that portion of the Colorado River and the canyon walls up to the 1,221-foot-above-sea-level contour. The artificial lake also drowned several large rapids, including Separation, where three of Powell's men refused to go any farther downriver in 1869.

Overleaf: (*Photo © by Dick Dietrich.*)

Glen Canyon Dam, which forms Lake Powell, sits immediately upstream of the Grand Canyon and has had profound effects upon the Colorado River's ecology. (Photo © by Gary Ladd.)

One small native cottonwood grows in the midst of the exotic tamarisk, a plant introduced into the Southwest around the turn of the century. (Photo © by Gary Ladd.)

This huge body of water evaporates six hundred thousand acre-feet per year, more than the Front Range communities of Colorado take from the river.

Other dams below Hoover soon followed, but their ecological impact on the riverine environment was not anticipated. The great conservationist Aldo Leopold had canoed the Colorado River delta in the predam days of 1922 and was struck by the unbelievable richness of life: "Fleets of cormorants drove their black prows in quest of skittering mullets; avocets, willets, and yellowlegs dozed one-legged on the bars; mallards, widgeons, and teal sprang skyward in alarm" (*A Sand County Almanac*). He did not know that within two decades the wildlife would be gone.

And the wildlife did not suffer alone. Cocopa Indians farming on the lower Colorado had also benefited from the annual spring flooding and renewal of the silt, a situation reminiscent of the Egyptian farmers along the Nile. The Cocopas had adapted their life style to accommodate the natural cycle of the river's flow. When the life-giving flow was interrupted, the delta turned into a desolate mud flat. The Cocopas could no longer irrigate their crops. Like the tumbleweed, both wildlife and human life blew away in the hot, dry desert wind.

The river was to lose its freedom upstream of the Grand Canyon as well. Fifteen miles above Lee's Ferry, a seven-hundred-foot-high concrete plug was constructed. The dam's gates closed in 1963, impounding water to form Lake Powell and drowning one the most beautiful canyons in the Southwest—Glen, "the canyon no one knew."

The amount of water released from Glen Canyon Dam is determined by the power needs of Phoenix, Las Vegas, and Los Angeles. Additional dams were, and occasionally still are, considered for the Grand Canyon itself. One site proposed is in the Marble Canyon section (at river mile 29.0 or an alternate at 32.2); the other is the Bridge Canyon or Hualapai Dam Site (river mile 236.3).

Glen Canyon Dam suddenly changed the water's color from silt red to clear green and controlled the volume of the river, but the extent of physical and ecological impacts on the Grand Canyon would not be recognized for some time.

Powell and his men had braved the river and its rapids in the name of science and exploration. For almost a hundred years, few dared repeat their voyage. As Glen Canyon Dam was being built, thousands took boat trips through Glen to see what would be lost. Boating interest spilled over to the Grand Canyon. Within a few years, more than fifteen thousand people per year were making the passage. The popularity of river running was increasing dramatically. The park service and conservationists became alarmed at the condition of the beaches along the river after a season of thousands of boaters. A series of studies were initiated to document the impact of river running and to help formulate a management plan.

These studies ran the gamut from inventorying the biotic resources of the river and riparian zone (river bank) to mapping the locations of campsites to investigating the sociological aspects of river running. Idealists wished for a magic number of river users that could be applied so the integrity of the river and canyon could be maintained. But life isn't that simple.

The sociologists, for example, began with the premise that as the number of river runners increased, the less satisfied they would be with their wilderness experience—a reasonable assumption about overcrowding. Surprisingly, though, the preliminary findings did not support the premise.

When the sociologists divided the river runners into two groups—those who were repeat customers versus first-timers—the mystery was solved. People who had made more than one river trip were indeed unhappy about the increasing crowds of people they met along the river on each succeeding descent. Sociologists term this phenomenon the Last Settler Syndrome; that is, people have a basic desire for pleasant experiences not to differ from their first encounter. The first-timers, however, generally

Since the building of Glen Canyon Dam, introduced rainbow trout have grown to prodigious lengths near Lee's Ferry. Since the cold river was poor invertebrate habitat, what the fish were feeding on was a mystery. Apparently, the trout are able to thrive on lipid oils found in diatoms (microscopic algae) attached to the abundant spinach-green Cladophora algae. (Photo © by Ron Sanford.)

The majestic golden eagle is an uncommon permanent resident in the Grand Canyon and can sometimes be seen soaring out over the Tonto Platform in search of squirrels or rabbits. (Photo © by Erwin & Peggy Bauer.)

Over one hundred pairs of endangered peregrine falcons currently nest along the Colorado River corridor within the Grand Canyon where a decade ago only a few lived. Biologists believe the dramatic increase in the falcon's numbers is related to changes in the riparian vegetation brought on by the Glen Canyon Dam regulating the flow of the river. (Photo © by Jeff Wiles.)

had a wonderful trip no matter how many other groups they encountered. Records show that the vast majority of people going down the Colorado are first-timers, and that this will probably be their only Colorado River trip. Hence the dilemma for the park service managers: Do they cater to the relatively small group of repeat boaters or to the majority of people who will float the river only once in a lifetime?

The research biologists, too, had difficulty calculating a specific carrying capacity for the riverine environment. After studying various impacts on vegetation, wildlife, and the river habitat, the researchers identified certain ecologically sensitive areas and specific visitor practices—walking off-trail, burning driftwood, dumping charcoal and sewage on beach areas—that could be mitigated by teaching people what to do properly. Ironically, some implemented solutions have created new problems. For example, river trips are now required to carry out all human fecal waste, but sanitary landfills outside the park are no longer accepting the estimated forty tons produced each year. One hundred people practicing "no trace" camping—being conscientious not to disturb the natural setting or inhabitants—would have little effect on a beach; however, just one careless person could wreak havoc. Again, no magic number.

In response to the studies' findings, the park service decided to maintain the number of users to near the 1974 levels, and to institute seminars and to require instruction on how to take care of the canyon for both commercial and private parties of river users. In actual numbers of people, the 1989 boating season witnessed about three thousand private and eighteen thousand commercial passengers. Departure schedules from Lee's Ferry are now designed in an attempt to reduce overcrowding. For the most part, impact from river runners has been significantly reduced.

During their time in the canyon, the biologists accidentally discovered other forces at work changing the natural ecosystem. The two major culprits were feral burros and Glen Canyon Dam.

FERAL BURROS

Over the past century, prospectors and canyon residents have on occasion lost or released livestock in the canyon. Cattle and horses do not fare well on their own and quickly die off. Not so with the hardy little burro. Burros not only survive, they thrive in the canyon, apparently feeding on nearly all available desert vegetation.

As early as the 1920s, park rangers were urging control measures to check the expanding burro herds. Chief Ranger J.P. Brooks wrote in 1932, "Overgrazed conditions exist on all areas ranged over by the burros." Between 1924 and 1969, almost three thousand burros were removed from Grand Canyon National Park. The removal policy was then halted in the belief that the burro problem had been eliminated.

While the biologists from the Museum of Northern Arizona were setting up study plots to examine the ecological impact by river runners, they noted that areas not used by people—areas that could be "control," or natural, sites—had been heavily trampled and overgrazed by burros. The fiesty burros would even eat the tops off the biologists' wooden survey stakes.

Studies were begun to document the damage caused by the feral burros. The biologists discovered that the Grand Canyon burros were rarely preyed upon, relatively free of disease, and that 80 percent of the jennies (females) one year or older were pregnant or lactating. With most females able to bear a colt every eighteen months, the burro population was estimated to be doubling every five to six years. This burgeoning burro population threatened not only the plants, but native animals, such as bighorn sheep.

Removal of these feral animals was not an easy task, however. A major hurdle to overcome was Public Law 92–195 passed by the U.S. Congress in 1972. This Wild Horse and Burro Act made it a felony to kill a feral burro on public lands. The designers of the bill were concerned about the disappearance of wild horses and burros from public lands; they felt these animals were symbols of our cultural and historical

Biologists recently discovered that bald eagles are now overwintering within the Grand Canyon in side-streams where introduced trout are spawning. (Photo © by Erwin & Peggy Bauer.)

heritage. A touching gesture—but the politicians did not realize the implications of having unmanaged herds.

A second problem facing the park service was that many tourists felt that the rangers were going after Brighty, the hero of Marguerite Henry's delightful children's book *Brighty of the Grand Canyon*. Well, maybe only a few people felt this way, but there was quite a public outcry over the park's initial plan to "remove" the burros by shooting them. In 1980, the park service agreed to let a private animal welfare group, The Fund for Animals, round up the burros. Some of the beasts were herded out trails, others were rafted out of the canyon, a few were helicoptered to the rim, and nearly six hundred burros were transported to a ranch in Texas. The Grand Canyon is now free of feral burros.

GLEN CANYON DAM

The Native Americans had their names for the river, and the Spanish conquistadors bestowed their own appellations, but it was Father Francisco Garces's *Rio Colorado* (Red River) that has become commonly accepted. The red color was the result of all the iron-oxide-stained silt, sand, and mud being transported by the flowing water.

In the past, perhaps more than five hundred million tons of sediment flowed through the canyon in a year. At the Bright Angel gaging station, as much as an incredible 27.6 million tons of suspended matter has passed in a single day.

After 1963, Glen Canyon Dam changed all of that. All of the sediment now settles on the bottom of Lake Powell. The river below Glen Canyon Dam runs clear (except when side-canyons below the dam flood and wash in sediment), jade green (the color caused primarily by algae), and cold (since water released by the dam is drawn from the dark depths of the lake). The average annual flow has been reduced to a third of its predam days.

No longer do annual spring floods scour away riverside vegetation and lie in new beaches. The sandy beaches are disappearing, eroding away, leaving only the heavier river cobbles or bedrock. Some geologists predict that, at the present rate of erosion, the beaches will be gone within two hundred years. The beaches that still exist are often choked by jungles of exotic tamarisk and native arrowweed and coyote willow.

Concern over the impacts of the dam and its operation led to the Glen Canyon Environmental Studies, a combined effort of the Bureau of Reclamation, U.S. Geological Survey, National Park Service, U.S. Department of Energy, Arizona Game and Fish Department, and private consultants. The studies were to determine the impacts of Glen Canyon Dam operations on the environmental and recreational resources of the Colorado River downstream in the fifteen miles of Glen Canyon National Recreation Area and 277 river miles of Grand Canyon National Park.

The Glen Canyon Environmental Studies found "positive" impacts to include the growth of a new riparian habitat, development of an exceptional trout fishery, and an extended whitewater boating season (an assertion disputed by some boaters).

Now that the annual scouring floods of spring have been eliminated, a number of plants have quickly invaded the river's edges producing a new riparian community. Besides the native arrowweed, seep-willow, and coyote willow, the exotic tamarisk is also abundant. Tamarisk, or salt cedar, was introduced into southern California and first reported along the Colorado River in the 1930s. It became widespread during the next thirty years, but was limited in abundance. The dam changed all of that. When mature, this fast-growing plant may produce as many as six hundred thousand tiny seeds a year, which are easily carried by the wind. Tamarisk also produces large quantities of leaf litter—litter that encourages fires that kill native species but not the hardy tamarisk—its roots simply re-sprout new growth. The leaves of the tamarisk also secrete salt, which inhibits germination and establishment of non-salt-tolerant species.

This new riparian community has been a boon for certain types of wildlife. Some species of birds, such as Bell's vireo, now nest in the

Canyon wall reflections. (Photo © by Ron Sanford.)

canyon because of the new habitat. Yellow-breasted chats, Lucy's and yellow warblers, summer tanagers, willow flycatchers, northern and hooded orioles, common yellowthroats, house finches, indigo and lazuli buntings, and blue grosbeaks have all increased in numbers, in some cases fivefold, along the river.

Indirectly, the dam may also be beneficial to the canyon's peregrine falcons, an endangered species. An apparent increase in riparian flying insects has led to more white-throated swifts and violet-green swallows, both favorite prey of the falcon. In their 1987 book *Grand Canyon Birds,* ornithologists Bryan Brown, Steve Carothers, and Roy Johnson state that "only a few breeding sites are known" for the peregrine falcon. But intensive surveys over the last couple of years have located over one hundred pairs of falcons in the canyon, most of them along the river corridor. Carothers feels the increased numbers of swifts and swallows—and any other birds foolish enough to fly across the river—keep the falcons well fed.

But not all riparian species have benefited.

Cliff swallows, for example, need mud for building nests, and this material is now in short supply. A decrease in their numbers has been noted.

The clear, cold water of the Colorado River has been detrimental to the native fish that were adapted to breeding in warm water. Of the eight native species, four—bonytail chub, roundtail chub, Colorado River squawfish, and razorback sucker—have been completely wiped out. There is new speculation, however, that channel catfish and carp, both introduced to the Colorado in the 1900s, may have played a significant role in the disappearance of the native fish.

Surprisingly, the "new" river system has proven beneficial to introduced rainbow trout. Trout near Lee's Ferry have grown to prodigious lengths, establishing this area as a nationally famous blue-ribbon fishery. But what are the trout feeding on? The cold river is a poor invertebrate habitat. The only apparent food source is the algae *Cladophora glomerata;* but trout are carnivores—or are they? Biologist Bill Leibfried explains: "My experiments have shown the

If river runners practiced "no-trace" camping—conscientious camping that does not disturb the natural environment—there would be little effect on the Colorado River's beaches; however, just one careless person could wreak havoc. (Photo © by Stewart Aitchison.)

trout are able to utilize lipid oils in diatoms [microscopic algae] attached to the filamentous *Cladophora* algae which is undigestible."

Fifty-two river miles downstream from Lee's Ferry, where the large tributary canyon of Nankoweap enters from the west, rainbow trout have taken up residence in the mouth of Nankoweap Creek. Since the mid-1980s, migrating bald eagles have discovered this new food source.

During the late winter and early spring of 1990, a team of biologists spent six weeks observing the bald eagles at Nankoweap. They found about fifteen hundred trout spawning in Nankoweap Creek, and twenty-six bald eagles feeding on about fifty fish per day. Four golden eagles were also taking advantage of the concentrated food source, making this the first documented instance of golden eagles fishing. According to team director Steve Carothers, "It's only a matter of time until the bald eagles take up breeding residence" in the Grand Canyon.

The Glen Canyon Environmental Studies also concluded that the dam has lengthened the boating season. In the predam days, flows ranged from a mere trickle of 750 cubic feet per second (cfs) to a terrifying 300,000 cfs, both of which are unboatable for most people. The dam has eliminated these record extremes as well as the seasonal extremes of spring floods and late summer lows. Thus, many boaters consider the Colorado River to be runnable year-round.

From the report's "negative" findings came predictions that flood releases (i.e. discharges greater than maximum power-plant releases of 31,500 cfs) could be expected about once every four years and would scour away riparian vegetation and beach sand. During the study, an exceptionally wet winter followed by a sudden thaw forced the release of 93,000 cfs in 1983. This flooding caused up to half of the riparian vegetation to be removed in some areas; 95 percent of the marshes along the river were destroyed; and 75 percent of the area's bird nests were lost. Canada geese and other shore-nesting birds have apparently abandoned the canyon.

Other negative impacts are caused by the

daily fluctuations in the river level. Except during periods of very high water, releases from the dam may vary on an hourly basis, often with two peaks and two troughs in a single day. The river level can change up to thirteen vertical feet in a twelve-hour period—all a result of changing power needs in distant cities. These wild fluctuations sweep away fish eggs, strand fish, reduce habitat for larval fishes, expose spawning beds, and may limit fish access to side-streams. Low flows may allow an increase in striped bass migrating upstream from Lake Mead. (Bass have already been reported as far upstream as Stone Creek.) These voracious predators could easily wipe out any remaining native fish species.

Glen Canyon Environmental Studies also suggested that a state of dynamic equilibrium had almost been reached in the bottom of the river channel prior to the 1983 flood. But the flood, plus increased daily fluctuations due to increased hydroelectric power demands, have renewed beach erosion.

Ironically, since silt is now filtered out by Glen Canyon Dam, phosphorus, which is attached to the silt particles and necessary for algae production, never reaches Lake Mead. The algae that would have been produced is fed upon by plankton, which in turn feeds threadfin shad, a staple of bass. Lake Mead has to be fertilized to keep its trophy sport fishery alive.

The five-year Glen Canyon Environmental Studies did not result in immediate action to limit damage to the canyon but rather, if you will excuse the pun, spawned more studies, this time in the form of two environmental impact statements. Secretary of the Interior Manuel Lujan has directed the Bureau of Reclamation to prepare an environmental impact study "to determine the impact of operations of the Glen Canyon Dam on the downstream ecological and environmental resources within the Grand Canyon National Park and the Glen Canyon National Recreation Area." (Sound familiar? See the purpose of the original study above.) A draft is expected during 1991.

In the fall of 1989, Utah Federal District Judge J. Thomas Greene ruled against the Department of Energy's Western Area Power Administration in a lawsuit filed by the National Wildlife Federation, the Grand Canyon Trust, and rafting groups. Greene found that WAPA's sales of Glen Canyon Dam power had clearly caused "irreparable injury" to the Grand Canyon river corridor. He revoked several recent WAPA contracts and told the agency to write an environmental impact statement on how its power sales affect the canyon.

Because of the daily fluctuations of the river flow, some scientists feel that each day is equivalent to a year's worth of impact. Therefore, a five-year study would equal almost two thousand years of impact! While the environmental impact statements are being prepared, the National Park Service has called for interim minimum flows of at least five thousand cfs.

According to Bob Witzeman, conservation chair of the Maricopa Audubon society in Phoenix, the policy of the Bureau of Reclamation and the Western Area Power Administration has been to let the water level rise behind the dam and then release large quantities during peak power demand in order to keep rates low for "preferred customers," namely, public power districts and irrigators. The power used by irrigators to pump groundwater is purchased at one-sixth the cost paid for privately generated power. Much of this water is used for the production of surplus crops that the federal government either subsidizes with price supports or pays other farmers not to produce. Hydropower is taking precedent over ecological integrity and recreation.

Dave Wegner, director of the Glen Canyon Environmental Studies, summed up the situation at a recent meeting of the Colorado River Guides Association: "I don't want to study the Grand Canyon to death. I want to go in and get good data as fast as possible so that we can mitigate impact as soon as possible. . . . We have to start managing the river as the system it is; just like Powell said we should."

Sensual fluted rock near Mile 232 Rapid. (Photo © by Ralph Lee Hopkins, Wilderland Images.)

Small, hidden springs, such as this one in Fern Glen Canyon, provide habitat for maidenhair ferns, mosses, and monkey-flowers. (Photo © by Rick McClain.)

FLORA AND FAUNA

Understandably, geologists were the first scientists drawn to the Grand Canyon. Biologists, botanists, and other natural scientists soon followed, however, eager to discover and document the unique and diverse plant and animal life awaiting them.

The first specific biological expedition to the central part of Grand Canyon was conducted by C. Hart Merriam, of the U.S. Biological Survey, and his assistant, Vernon Bailey. Merriam and Bailey were in northern Arizona as part of a broader study, ostensibly to shed light on the economic (primarily agricultural) importance of the biotic resources of an area encompassing a "diversity of physical and climatic conditions, particularly . . . a high mountain." The San Francisco Peaks just north of Flagstaff had been chosen because of their "southern position, isolation, great altitude, and proximity to an arid desert."

Merriam and Bailey had established their main camp at Little Spring at the northwest base of the San Francisco Peaks. On September 9, 1889, they headed toward the Grand Canyon taking the "usual road." This two-day route went from Little Spring to Hull Spring to Red Horse Tank and then to another tank (a natural depression that catches run-off to form a pond) known as Cañon Spring.

From Cañon Spring, Merriam and Bailey descended the Old Hance Trail to spend two days and nights within the canyon. Merriam found the cactus mice to be "excessively abundant," later recalling: "During the two nights spent in the canyon, these mice came about my blanket in great numbers and I was forced to place my scanty stock of provisions in a small tree for protection; but even there it was not safe, for the mice are excellent climbers, and I shot one by moonlight as it peered down at me from a low branch." But mice weren't Merriam's only nocturnal visitors. "I was awakened at midnight by a sniffling noise about my head. Rising suddenly on my elbow, a small animal scampered hurriedly away over the rocks. His form was only dimly outlined in the dark, but a hasty shot left no doubt as to his identity, and a moment later I held in my hand the type of a new species of Little Striped Skunk."

The work he had done in the canyon, on the San Francisco Peaks, and out in the Painted Desert led Merriam to formulate his now-famous "Life Zone" concept of plant and animal communities being distributed on the basis of temperature. Simply put, as you ascend in elevation, the temperature decreases, and the flora and fauna change as though you were traveling north in latitude. Merriam recognized various life zones ranging from Sonoran-type desert at the bottom of the Grand Canyon to alpine tundra at the summit of the San Francisco Peaks— a horizontal distance of about eighty miles and

Evening primrose carpet a beach near Nevill's Rapid. The flowers open in the evening and are pollinated by night-flying insects. Each blossom lasts just one night. (Photo © by Gary Ladd.)

Above: *One of the first biologists to venture into the Grand Canyon was C. Hart Merriam in 1889. His investigations there and around the San Francisco Peaks near Flagstaff led him to formulate his "Life Zone" concept, which states that plant and animal distribution is governed by temperature. (Photo reproduced courtesy of Museum of Northern Arizona.)* **Below**: *Two hundred seventy million years ago, great desert dunes marched across northern Arizona. Cross-bedding in the Coconino Sandstone is one clue to its eolian origin. (Photo © by Betty Crowell.)*

COCONINO SANDSTONE
(PERMIAN AGE)

THE SLOPING SURFACES OF THIS SAND INDICATE THAT
IT WAS PROBABLY DEPOSITED IN DUNES BY THE WIND.

a vertical change of ten thousand feet. Biologically, it was like going from northern Mexico to northern Canada.

Other biologists soon called attention to other environmental constraints—such as precipitation and composition of the substrate—that affect biotic communities, but Merriam clung steadfastly to his original idea that temperature alone was the most important factor. Although his dogmatic position ultimately proved incorrect, Merriam is still given credit for encouraging biologists to consider the role of environment upon the makeup of plant and animal communities.

One hundred years after Merriam, my friend Bill and I start down the Kaibab Trail, one of only two maintained rim-to-river trails off of the South Rim. We quickly descend in a series of steep switchbacks through the Kaibab Limestone. On the rim, pinyon pine and juniper had dominated, but here on this shaded slope grow a number of tall, Christmas-tree-shaped Douglas firs, whose roots tenaciously grip the shallow, steep soil.

These north-facing slopes near the rim often harbor a few descendants of the Douglas fir or white fir forests that blanketed the upper rim areas during the Ice Age. Besides these Pleistocene relicts, scientists have uncovered other clues to past environments, sometimes in as unlikely a place as a pack rat nest.

To most people, an old pack rat nest—a midden of twigs and rat droppings all glued together with resinlike urine (a process scientifically called *induration*) and tucked under an overhang—is a fairly disgusting sight. To the paleobotanist, however, who delights in the study of ancient plants, these piles of rat dung are like a crystal ball to plant life of the past. Amazingly, some of these nests have been radiocarbon-dated at ten thousand or more years old. By analyzing the plant pollen and plant parts stuck in these nests, the paleobotanist can deduce what plants were growing in the area thousands of years ago. Knowing the specific vegetation types, the scientist can then speculate on the ancient climatic conditions.

As we travel along our downward trail, especially through the limestone layers, we notice an occasional cave—caves that have yielded further evidence of past Grand Canyon environments. Rampart Cave in western Grand Canyon, for example, served as a bathroom for the now-extinct Shasta ground sloth, a bearlike creature and distant relative of the armadillo. The dry cave preserved the fecal matter so well that a sample sent to be radiocarbon-dated was tossed away by a technician who thought someone was playing a crude joke by sending a fresh-smelling specimen. Another sample that followed was dated at more than ten thousand years old. As with the pack rat nest, pollen and plant parts could also be recovered and studied. Results showed that the sloth had been feeding on globemallow, Mormon tea, and common reed, all plants found in the Grand Canyon region today.

Caves have also yielded bones of former canyon residents. Extinct species of mammoth, Harrington's mountain goat—a white-haired animal similar to the modern mountain goat, but smaller and of slightly different body proportions—a camel-like creature, a burrolike creature, and a giant carrion-feeding bird (*Teratornis merriami*) once inhabited the area. California condor remains indicate that these impressive birds once lived here, too. (Some scientists would like to reintroduce endangered condors to the Grand Canyon.)

When these creatures first inhabited the Grand Canyon some thirty thousand years ago, there was a juniper woodland near the river where today there is desert. Pinyon pine had not yet reached the canyon. Instead, spruce, fir, and limber pine made up the rim forest. Surprisingly, there is no evidence of the intermediate ponderosa pine forest so prevalent in northern Arizona today. The dominant large mammal was Harrington's goat, which had an omnivorous diet ranging from various shrubs to spruce. Temperatures were less extreme than they are today; summers were cooler, and the majority of precipitation came during the winter months.

The Utah agave is a member of the amaryllis family. Occasionally, hikers in the Grand Canyon will come upon old dugout pits in the ground where Havasupai or Paiutes roasted these plants for food. (Photo © by Ralph Lee Hopkins, Wilderland Images.)

Although rarely seen, desert millipedes are actually fairly common but spend most of their time underground awaiting summer rains. (Photo © by Tom Brownold.)

Between 10,900 and 11,300 years ago, there were mass extinctions of many Pleistocene birds and mammals, including such apparently ecologically successful species as Harrington's goat. What was the cause? Was it the warming and drying trend that began to affect the Southwest at that time? Was it the invasion of a new, very efficient, very human predator? or a combination of factors? The research and debate continue, but regardless of the cause, by 8,500 years ago, the modern canyon flora and fauna communities had been established.

As we continue our hike, the trail switchbacks lengthen through the cross-bedded Coconino Sandstone down to the relatively flat Cedar Ridge, but no true cedars are here. Cowboys often called the fragrant juniper by that name.

Among the junipers around us, two deceptively similar plants are growing. Both have stiff, pointed leaves emerging in a basal rosette. One is the banana yucca, a member of the lily family and one of the most useful plants to Native Americans. It provided soap from its roots, fiber from its leaves, and food from its fruit.

The yucca can be, if weather conditions permit, a perennial bloomer. Soft, creamy yellow flowers on a two-foot-high stalk attract Pronubid moths to form a symbiotic relationship. The female moth gathers pollen from various blossoms until she has a large ball of it under her head. She then enters another flower, inserts her ovipositor into the plant's pistil, or female part, and lays her eggs. During this process, the moth rubs some of the pollen onto the flower's stigma, or male part, insuring development of seed production, which will feed her young. The larvae eat only a portion of the seeds produced, thus new yuccas may germinate from the "surplus" seeds.

The other plant is a Utah agave, a member of the amaryllis family. Although commonly called century plant, this species blooms when it is fifteen to twenty-five years old, not one hundred

Many varieties of lizard roam the canyon walls. (Photo © by Michael Francis.)

years old. They store up energy in the form of carbohydrates in their bases, until one spring day, they begin to send up stalks. At first the stalk grows only two to three inches per day, but eventually—provided a rock squirrel doesn't nibble the tender shoot—it races skyward, adding ten inches per day, until it reaches a height of ten feet or more. The upper stalk bears beautiful yellow flower clusters. After pollination, the entire plant dies, but lives on through its seed and nearby vegetatively produced clones.

From Cedar Ridge, our trail skirts the base of O'Neill Butte and passes the last of the junipers. In a sense, in the Grand Canyon, you descend to the timberline.

We stop for a rest in the shade of a Supai Sandstone ledge. Toward the back of this little overhang, seemingly random strands of cobweb stretch several feet between the roof and the ground. Fluffy, windblown seeds, pieces of dried leaves, and old insect exoskeletons adorn the untidy web. These unremarkable webs are spun by black widow spiders, a very common desert resident. Black widows tend to be nocturnal, so you probably won't see one unless you're in the habit of poking around shallow caves and overhanging cliffs in the dark.

As I look down, I notice a number of small holes penetrating the sandy soil beneath a nearby shrub. Each hole is surrounded by soft, earth pellets about the size of tapioca balls—the distinctive sign of millipedes. Also under that bush is a sun-bleached snail shell—a creature given the euphonious scientific name *Oreohelix*. What are these "garden creatures" doing here in the desert?

Desert millipedes are actually quite common in arid regions. They spend much of their lives underground in cooler, damper soil, patiently waiting for a summer rainstorm before emerging to ingest soil and feed on decomposing vegetation. Land snails can live within rock slides or under vegetation, such as the dried, fallen leaves of an agave. When cool, wet weather per-

Formerly called cryptogamic crust, this dark microbiotic crust is composed of cyanobacteria, green algae, soil lichens, mosses, bacteria, and fungi. This remarkable crust not only protects the friable desert soil from erosion, but also aids in increasing the nitrogen content and that of other nutrients for the benefit of other plants. (Photo © by Gary Ladd.)

mits, these mollusks emerge and forage. For many desert denizens, life consists of patiently waiting for a brief period of sex and eating during rare damp weather.

As we continue our descent, the next geologic layer that we pass is the Redwall Limestone, which forms a persistent cliff through the canyon some four to six hundred feet high. This formation is one of the major barriers to rim-to-river travel. In the hundreds of miles of its exposure, only about 150 routes are known where it is possible to walk or scramble through. Many of these passages were discovered by one man—Harvey Butchart—who has been exploring every corner of the Grand Canyon for nearly a half-century.

In 1945, Harvey Butchart arrived in Flagstaff to begin a teaching career at Arizona State College (now Northern Arizona University). This was his first time in the Southwest and his fateful introduction to the Grand Canyon. At first his hikes were casual forays along the well-known trails, but as Butchart learned more about the canyon's history, he explored old, abandoned trails and tried to trace other forgotten routes. Of the 150 or so named buttes within the canyon, Butchart has scaled more than eighty of them. Butchart's three little guidebooks to hiking in the Grand Canyon contain a wealth of information. Now in his eighties, Butchart is spending his retirement scouting out new sections of the Grand Canyon.

The Redwall cliff before us is pockmarked with solution caves. These caves are tunnels—now exposed by erosion—which were formed as groundwater slowly dissolved the limestone along joints, bedding planes, and faults. In certain areas of the canyon—like Vasey's Paradise, Roaring Springs, and Thunder River—water still issues forth in wonderful cascading falls.

At the base of the Redwall and the underlying Muav cliffs, our trail again flattens a bit. We cross the Tonto Platform, which is dotted with woody blackbrush, a tough, desert member of

This five-inch giant hairy scorpion may be intimidating but actually is less dangerous than the much smaller bark scorpion. Scorpions are rarely seen unless you habitually poke under rocks and dead vegetation. (Photo © by Glenn Randall.)

the rose family. Instead of continuing down to the Colorado River, we find the less-used trail leading west over to Pipe Creek.

Several older trails seem to parallel the one we are following. A major problem in the Grand Canyon, and in many other desert areas, is multiple-trailing. Different people, and animals such as burros, often take different paths to reach their destinations. At first this activity seems harmless, but in arid regions, the desert soils are quite fragile and friable.

If you get down close to ground level, you will see a darkish crust on the dirt. This crust is composed of a remarkable community dominated by cyanobacteria (formerly called blue-green algae) living with green algae, soil lichens, mosses, bacteria, and fungi—collectively called microbiotic crust. (Other references may call it cryptogamic crust, but this term refers only to the community of nonvascular plants—mosses, lichens, and green algae.)

This bumpy surface interrupts wind patterns, reduces wind erosion, and traps windborne soil particles. The microbiotic crust physically protects the soil from rain erosion, decreases evaporation of moisture, and enhances seed germination. The cyanobacteria and green algae also help enrich the soil by taking atmospheric nitrogen and concentrating it in the crust. This crust is the key factor in stabilizing desert soils and increasing the soil's supply of nutrients. Unfortunately, a few footsteps, hoof prints, or tire tracks, and the crust may be destroyed.

Renee Beymer, a graduate student from Arizona State University, has studied the effects of grazing on microbiotic crust in the pinyon-juniper woodland in the Grand Canyon. Although most of her study areas have been free of livestock grazing for fifty years, the crust is just now recovering.

Near the river where river runners and feral burros have caused multiple-trailing, Kim Crumbo, a park service resource management specialist, has been attempting to revegetate

In 1937 the American Museum of Natural History mounted an expedition to the top of Shiva Temple to learn if unique animals existed on its isolated summit. While the biologists did not discover any new species, the news media had a heyday claiming the scientists were going to find dinosaurs on the "lost world" of Shiva Temple. (Photo reproduced courtesy of Department of Library Services, American Museum of Natural History.)

some of the extraneous paths. Since planting living desert shrubs is difficult at best, Kim has come up with the innovative idea of planting dead plants. He explains, "You don't have to water, and the dead bushes help stabilize the soil and provide shade for seedlings to germinate."

From under a nearby blackbrush, a poorwill flies up, does several slow, deep wingbeats, and comes to rest in the shade of another bush. Poorwills are rarely seen during the day. More commonly, they shoot up in front of your headlights as you travel desert dirt roads at night; or you may have heard one's plaintive call on a quiet summer evening. The bird's ancient Hopi name, *holchko,* translates as "old man who sleeps in winter"—a very appropriate description. The poorwill's "whiskers" give it an "old man" appearance, and it is one of the few birds that can hibernate.

Tonight we camp at Pipe Creek near the ruins of an old ranger patrol cabin. Like Merriam be-

fore us, we are troubled with pesty rodents looking for a handout—several representatives of the five species of white-footed mice that reside in the canyon. A rustling in my pack wakes me up. I reach for my flashlight and aim it toward the noise. A long fluffy tail ringed with black-and-white stripes cascades out of my backpack. The ringtail cat is having a great time tearing into my food bag.

The light startles the creature and it backs out. A foxlike face topped with large pointed ears squints in my direction. The slender body looks sinfully soft and plush and invites stroking, but as I rise up on an elbow, the cat vanishes into the dark. Just as well, since these relatives of the raccoon have very sharp teeth.

Dawn comes much too early. After a simple breakfast of granola bars, fruit, and coffee, I proceed to shake out my boots before wrestling them on. Usually the only thing to fall out of them is the sand and pebbles accumulated the day before. But this morning a five-inch-long,

Within the Grand Canyon is a unique race of the prairie rattlesnake with the appropriate scientific name of Crotalus viridis abussus. *The Grand Canyon rattlesnake is usually salmon-pink to vermilion in color, but can also be light tan. Since this snake is seldom encountered, little information is available regarding the effects or frequency of bites from this snake. The only person I know of who was bitten recovered fully. (Photo © by Glenn Randall.)*

A western tiger swallowtail butterfly visits a thistle in Saddle Canyon. (Photo © by John Macfarlane.)

straw-colored, stiffly moving scorpion tumbles out.

Arizona is home for thirty species of scorpions, but only one is considered deadly. The bark scorpion, *Centruroides sculpturatus,* lives in the Grand Canyon and can inject a neurotoxin venom. The large specimen in my boot is the giant hairy, *Hadrurus hirsutus,* which can deliver a painful sting, but is not deadly like its smaller relative. The ancestors of scorpions crept from the Silurian seas some four hundred million years ago and have changed little since—making them an evolutionary success story.

Biologists have long been looking for evolutionary evidence within the great canyon. On the far side of the Colorado River, Shiva Temple, rises as an isolated mesa within the canyon. The flat, forested mesa top is even with the North Rim, but separated from it by a deep notch. In 1937, Harold E. Anthony of the American Museum of Natural History mounted a much publicized expedition to the top of Shiva Temple hoping to perhaps discover unique subspecies or races of rodents that had been isolated from their North Rim relatives for millions of years. The news media, however, blew the whole study effort out of proportion. Reporters began to call Shiva the "lost world," even suggesting that dinosaurs still roamed the summit.

For ten days, the scientists collected and examined small mammals, finding no substantial differences between Shiva's individuals and those of the rims. The general public was disappointed, but the expedition shed new light on the question of how isolated Shiva Temple was to mammals. Anthony noted: "We did not expect to find dinosaurs; we did not find them. We may have been several thousand years too early to find tangible evidence of evolutionary changes; these will most certainly appear sooner or later."

However, the Grand Canyon *is* a barrier to some creatures. The best-known example is the Kaibab squirrel on the North Rim and its cousin, the Abert, on the South Rim. Both are closely linked to the ponderosa pine forest and find it impossible to descend into the desert habitats of the inner canyon. Different species or subspecies, but ecological equivalents, of coyote, spotted skunk, woodrat, porcupine, chipmunk, and pocket mice are found on either side of the Colorado River. Presumably their ancestors, too, became separated as the canyon deepened and similar habitats became isolated from each other.

For some creatures, the Grand Canyon acts as a refugium, an isolated locale where unique or endemic species have evolved. The most famous example is the Grand Canyon rattlesnake. Park naturalist Edwin D. McKee collected a pink-colored rattlesnake on the Tanner Trail a few hundred feet below the South Rim in 1929. This snake proved to be a unique race of the widespread prairie rattler. Snake expert L. M. Klauber christened the new form *Crotalus viridis abyssus.*

Less intimidating but no less fascinating than a rattlesnake are several species of butterflies native to the Grand Canyon—pegala satyr (*Cercyonis pegala damei*), Grand Canyon ringlet (*Coenonympha ochracea furcae*), and Grand Canyon swallowtail (*Papilio indra kaibabensis*). The lepidopterists believe that the ringlet is found only in meadows along the South Rim. Not even one pair of these delicate insects has ever been blown to the north side on a windy day and taken up permanent residence!

Given the rugged topography and span of environments of the Grand Canyon, it's not to difficult to understand how plants and animals can become isolated and slowly evolve into unique species. More difficult to explain, however, are species such as the semiaquatic water bug that is found only in the Grand Canyon *and* in the mountains of central Mexico. Obviously, biogeographers have a lot of work ahead of them.

Bill and I finally reach Indian Gardens located on the busy Bright Angel Trail. An apocryphal story relates how in 1913 former President Teddy Roosevelt descended the Bright Angel Trail on his way to the North Rim for a hunting excursion. There were still a few Havasupai In-

Overleaf: *Mule-train on Bright Angel Trail. (Photo © by Dick Dietrich.)*

The 1904 Kolb Studio is perched on the very edge of the South Rim. Emery and Ellsworth Kolb were early-day residents and photographers at the Grand Canyon. Until his death in 1976, Emery showed his 1911 film of a Colorado River trip daily to canyon visitors. (Photo © by S. Aitchison.)

dians living along Garden Creek, growing some corn and beans in the blazing sun. Roosevelt got off his mule, strolled over to these natives, introduced himself, and said, "Five years ago, I declared the Grand Canyon a national monument for the people of the nation. I'm afraid you folks will have to leave."

Today, large Fremont cottonwoods, transplanted from a grove twenty-four miles to the east, shade the Indian Gardens day-use area. The Havasupai, and perhaps earlier people, had been able to descend off the rim to this watering hole because of the Bright Angel Fault running the length of this short tributary canyon. This major fault has upthrown the west side of this tributary canyon about two hundred feet, breaking the otherwise continuous walls of Redwall Limestone and Coconino Sandstone. As erosion wid-

ened the fault into a canyon, stone rubble accumulated along the break forming a ramp of sorts that could be negotiated by sandaled feet. This rough path was later engineered into the mule and foot trail used today.

These ancient faults, so wonderfully displayed in the Grand Canyon, are not necessarily dormant. On March 4, 1989, two earthquakes shook the South Rim and the inner canyon. Rocks fell near the first tunnel on the Bright Angel Trail. There was minor damage to the historic Kolb Studio perched overlooking the trailhead, and dishes crashed to the floor at Phantom Ranch.

The canyon stirs, life evolves, and tiny humbled backpackers slowly plod up the trail. Merriam was correct in calling the Grand Canyon "a world in itself."

Desert wildflowers in June—a cheerful wash of color to the Grand Canyon scenery. (Photo © by Dick Dietrich.)

ROCKS AND FOSSILS

I pull up into the parking area at Lipan Point, one of my favorite South Rim viewpoints. Looking north, you can see the Colorado River meandering through a relatively broad valley. This is the widest, most open part of the Grand Canyon. The broad delta of Unkar Creek is easily visible. For nearly four hundred years, the Anasazi farmed Unkar's sandy terraces. Centuries of flash floods down Unkar Creek have pushed rocks into the Colorado forming a respectable rapid. Not far below Unkar, the river meets the somber, harder Precambrian rocks in which only a narrow gorge has been carved. Here, boulder-strewn Hance Rapid marks the entrance to the Inner Gorge. To the east of my viewpoint, the Painted Desert and the Navajo Country shimmer in rising heat waves. Behind us, the horizon is capped with the outline of the volcanic San Francisco Peaks, the highest mountains in Arizona, sacred to the Hopi, Navajo, and other Native Americans.

Just a few hundred yards east of Lipan Point begins an old prospector's trail, called Tanner's Trail. In 1880 Seth Tanner, a Mormon settler from Tuba City, located some minor copper and silver deposits in the Palisades Creek area. To reach these prospects, he and several other men improved an old Anasazi and Hopi trail from the South Rim.

Two years later, on the North Rim, subsequent explorers developed a northeastern route leading into the canyon. ". . . encamped in snow, often concealed for days in the driving frozen mist and whirling snow," John Wesley Powell and his crew "gradually overcame the apparently insurmountable obstacles" and upgraded an old Paiute route into Nankoweap Canyon. Then Powell led the eminent paleontologist Charles Doolittle Walcott to the Nankoweap Trail to study the rocks of eastern Grand Canyon. Walcott spent seventy-two days in the inner canyon. During that time he and his assistants trailblazed along a major fault that runs west of and is partly responsible for the row of isolated buttes—Nankoweap Mesa, Malgosa Crest, Kwagunt Butte, Awatubi Crest, Chuar Butte, and Temple Butte. He eventually reached the Unkar Creek area before retracing his steps back to the North rim.

Trails like the ones Tanner and Walcott marked led later prospectors, wanderers, outlaws, and—later—geologists into the canyon. In 1886, William Bass, an early South Rim resident, and two companions decided to search for gold supposedly hidden in the canyon by the infamous Mormon John D. Lee. (Lee led a group of Mormons in the murder of the adult members of a wagon train from Missouri. Lee hid out at a number of remote Arizona and Utah locations until he was finally captured, tried, and shot.) Bass and his friends had descended only a short distance on the Tanner Trail when they

Polished river boulders near Red Canyon. (Photo © by Les Manevitz.)

The large delta just left of Unkar Rapid was home to the prehistoric Anasazi. (Photo © by Les Manevitz.)

encountered five rough-looking hombres with eighteen horses. Bass had a pretty good hunch what these unsavory fellows were up to, but wisely chose to ignore the illegal activity.

For a number of years, horse thieves—such as those met by Bass and company—utilized Walcott's and Tanner's trails as a cross-canyon route. They would steal horses in Utah and drive them to Arizona to be sold. Horses stolen from Arizona or New Mexico would then be taken to Utah. It was hardly an easy way to make money. Not only was the trip long and arduous, but crossing the Colorado River could be fatal. More than one horse—and no doubt an occasional rider—fell off the precarious trails or was drowned by the river's swift current.

I wonder if the outlaws noticed the seashell fragments in the Kaibab Limestone. Did they puzzle over the animal tracks frozen in the Coconino Sandstone? Did they see the impression left by a giant fern frond in the Hermit Shale? As their horses kicked up dust going over the pass between Nankoweap Butte and Nankoweap Mesa, did these trail-hardened men ponder the origin of the odd-shaped stromatolite fossils common in boulders along the trail? Or were they ever fooled by the gold-colored spheres of iron pyrite eroding out of the ancient rocks?

Ever since Powell's first descent of the Colorado River in 1869, geologists have been attempting to piece together the puzzle of the Grand Canyon's geologic history. One of the first steps has been to examine the individual puzzle pieces—the distinctive layers of rock so clearly displayed in the walls of the canyon. The somber, dark rocks of the Inner Gorge are the oldest rocks exposed in the Grand Canyon and among the oldest exposed in North America. The great antiquity and deformation of these rocks makes their origin difficult to decipher. But much of the canyon's story can be told.

The Grand Canyon actually began some 2.5 to three billion years ago off the present coast of Peru. Tectonic plate movement has since "rafted" that part of the world to its present location in the American Southwest—a whole

other story in itself. An estimated six vertical miles of dark volcanic and sedimentary rocks accumulated over already existing metamorphic rocks. Over millions of years, the volcanic and sedimentary rocks were slowly pushed and folded, like a rug being kicked, resulting in the formation of a huge mountain range. The tremendous compression of the rocks caused them to change (metamorphose) into schist. The schist was broken by faults, and in places magma intruded and cooled into granite. By 1.7 billion years ago, the Vishnu Mountains were completed.

But as soon as mountains are born, erosion begins to wear them down. The Vishnu Mountains were reduced to an almost level plain. Small islands of schist persisted, surrounded by an ocean where sediments derived from these and more distant crumbling mountains accumulated.

From about 1.2 billion to eight hundred million years ago, these sediments continued to build up in layers with interbedded lavas, eventually totaling over three vertical miles in thickness. Geologists call these deposits the Grand Canyon Supergroup. About seven hundred million years ago, the Supergroup was stressed and broken into huge blocks by faulting. The blocks tilted ten to fifteen degrees, resulting in another mountain range; like the earlier Vishnu Mountains, these peaks were planed off by erosion. In some places, the Supergroup was completely erased.

This period of erosion stretched over an enormous amount of time until another sea invaded the area, depositing the Tapeats Sandstone about six hundred million years ago. Powell called the abrupt contact between the flat-lying Tapeats and the twisted, deformed Vishnu or between the Tapeats and the angled Supergroup the Great Unconformity.

All of this mountain building and destruction accounts for only those rocks seen near the bottom of the Grand Canyon. The history of the multicolored, horizontal layers of sedimentary rock that rise above the Inner Gorge to the rim is a fascinating story of changing environments

Fluted and polished Vishnu Schist along the Colorado River, the roots of ancient mountains some 1.7 billion years old. (Photo © by Gary Ladd.)

and evolving life forms.

From about six hundred million years ago until sixty or seventy million years ago, the region now known as the Colorado Plateau was often near or below sea level. Oceans transgressed and retreated, swamps were covered by dune deserts, the sea returned, and life evolved from simple marine invertebrates to fish, sharks, and reptiles.

When geologists examine the fossil record from the Grand Canyon Supergroup deposits to the overlying Tapeats Sandstone, they find an apparent "explosion" of life forms. About the only fossils seen in the older rocks are rounded colonies of cyanobacteria known as stromatolites. Yet the Tapeats and the overlying Bright Angel Shale record an advancing ocean teaming with an amazing diversity of complex, multicelled organisms—marine worms, brachiopods, and trilobites, to name a few. What transpired during the Great Unconformity timespan?

Biologists speculate that the giant step to multicelled organisms could not take place until oxygen became a major component of the atmosphere. Somewhere during the Precambrian era (three to four billion years ago), organic compounds transformed into the first living cells, termed *prokaryotes*. These single cells were types of bacteria and cyanobacteria living in a world lacking free oxygen; thus they were necessarily *anaerobic,* that is, not dependent upon free oxygen in the atmosphere. The cyanobacteria, however, practiced photosynthesis—the conversion of water vapor and carbon dioxide into the organic compounds needed for growth—and oxygen was a by-product. Over the next couple of billion years, oxygen slowly built up in the atmosphere. Lightning caused some of this oxygen to combine into ozone in the stratosphere. This ozone layer, some fifty miles up, filters out much of the sun's ultraviolet light, which is harmful to living things. The abundance of oxygen, the filtering effect of the ozone, and other changes to the environment set the stage for the development of organisms that could be *aerobic,* the oxygen-dependent *eukaryotes.*

Eukaryotes are membranous cells that repro-

Geologist John Wesley Powell named the contact between the lower, tilted Pre-Cambrian rocks and the upper, horizontal Paleozoic rocks the Great Unconformity. This angular meeting place represents a very long period of erosion (possibly over 300 million years) when ancient tilted mountains were beveled off before an invading sea deposited coarse sands. During this "missing time," life on earth dramatically evolved from simple single-celled organisms to a remarkably diverse collection of multicellular marine creatures such as worms, trilobites, and brachiopods. (Photo © by Ralph Lee Hopkins, Wilderland Images.)

duce by the division of a nucleus, the storeroom for genetic material. Prokaryotes reproduce simply by duplicating themselves into two equal parts—a very limited way of evolving new organisms. But with the eukaryotes continually shuffling their genetic material, the possible permutations were countless. Complex multicellular organisms formed for the first time, just as the last layers of the Grand Canyon Supergroup were being deposited. This possibility for some cells to be better adapted to their environment than others started the whole progression that Darwin would label "survival of the fittest." During the timespan that Powell called the Great Unconformity, evolution began full bore. Unfortunately, in the Grand Canyon region, it was a time of erosion rather than deposition, so there is no fossil record until the later marine Tapeats Sandstone. By then, an amazing array of life had developed.

All these incredibly ancient times and miraculous events make my head spin. I decide to stroll down the Tanner Trail a ways and hope that I don't run into any outlaws.

I sit down on a low wall of stacked flagstones to catch my breath. A side-blotched lizard does push-ups nearby to impress upon other lizards just whose territory this is. Across from me a large slab of the tan Coconino Sandstone rests on the slope. A set of well-defined fossil tracks march up the stone, a record of another reptile's passing some 270 million years ago.

Like several geologists before him, early park naturalist Eddie McKee wondered about the distinctive angled lines, called cross-bedding, coursing through the Coconino Sandstone and the ichnites (fossil tracks) that almost without exception climbed up these slopes but never down. His study and experiments led him to believe that the Coconino was actually petrified windblown (eolian) sand dunes from an ancient desert that covered northern Arizona and southern Utah, the cross-beds being layers or sand piled up by the wind.

The mystery of the uphill tracks was apparently solved when McKee performed an experiment with a chuckwalla. When the large lizard climbed a dune, and the sand was a little damp, a good set of tracks were imprinted. But when the lizard came down, its plunging gait did not produce the same neat impressions.

Not until thirty years later did anyone investigate further the origin of the fossil tracks in the Coconino. Leonard R. Brand, a geologist from Loma Linda University, performed experiments with several species of salamanders using dry sand, damp sand, wet sand, and underwater sand. McKee had not done any experiments using salamanders, having been told by a biologist that salamanders don't walk underwater. Brand made the startling discovery that the tracks left by a salamander walking up a dune underwater most closely resemble the fossilized tracks in the Coconino. Furthermore, the amphibian often swam off the top of the dune rather than walking down, thus accounting for the lack of downhill tracks. Therefore, Brand suggested that at least part of the Coconino— the bottom half of the formation where most of the fossil tracks are located—is not eolian at all but rather a water deposit. This controversial conclusion is not supported by other geologists who have closely examined the differences between wind- and water-caused cross-bedding. Perhaps further investigations are warranted.

I think about Tanner and the other hopeful prospectors of the late nineteenth century. The lucky few who located copper, silver, or lead were usually discovering these small deposits in features called breccia pipes. In the canyon, these pipes are formed when acidic subsurface water causes the roof of an underground cave (usually in the Redwall Limestone) to collapse. A vertical column or pipe is formed of breccia, broken rock that has become cemented together by the action of groundwater over millions of years. These pipes range from mere inches in diameter to more than three hundred feet across and thousands of feet in height. While less than 8 percent of the Grand Canyon area's breccia pipes contain valuable minerals, a few contain relatively high concentrations of uranium—a selectivity which confounds geologists.

Above: *The origin of fossil tracks in the Coconino Sandstone that almost always go up, and never down, bedding planes puzzled geologists until park naturalist Eddie McKee did an experiment. By placing a chuckwalla on a sand dune, McKee discovered that the lizard left a good set of uphill tracks; when it came down, however, its plunging gait did not produce neat impressions. (Photo © by Gary Ladd.)* **Below:** *Chuckwallas usually never venture far from a crevice. When threatened, this large lizard will wedge itself in a rock crevice and inflate its body, making itself almost impossible to remove without injury. Chuckwallas are vegetarians and were considered a food delicacy among the Paiute. (Photo © by Stewart Aitchison.)*

One of the earliest forms of life on earth was the stromatolite, a colony-forming cyanobacteria (formerly called blue-green algae but now considered a unique group of organisms). Some stromatolite fossils found in Grand Canyon rocks as old as a billion years look essentially the same as living colonies in the ocean today. (Photo © by Gary Ladd.)

Over a thousand breccia pipes have been discovered on the Hualapai Reservation, which includes part of the western Grand Canyon. Their economic potential is being examined, and the outcome could trigger new mining in the Grand Canyon.

From my rest stop along the Tanner Trail, I can scan all the layers of rock from rim to river. Even for me, a nongeologist, nature seems to have laid the entire geologic record at my feet. But not so—there are some pages missing. Besides the Great Unconformity, there are smaller unconformities between some of the horizontal sedimentary layers, periods of time when erosion rather than deposition was in progress. Over the last hundred years, geologists had come to assume that all of the remaining pages of the geologic story had been studied and described. Thus it came as quite a surprise when an entirely new layer was recently discovered in the Grand Canyon.

During the 1970s, geologist George Billingsley found cross-sections of ancient river valleys cut into the Redwall Limestone. The dark reddish brown rocks that later filled these valleys represent a twenty-million-year period that is missing from the rock record in other parts of the canyon.

This newly discovered deposit was appropriately named the Surprise Canyon Formation. According to Billingsley, it has yielded a greater variety of fossils than any other formation in the Grand Canyon. He has found shark's teeth, star-fish, brachiopods, blastoids (a starfish relative), corals, bryozoans (tiny colonial creatures), foraminifera (a type of protozoan), conodonts (common but mysterious toothlike and platelike fossils of unknown zoological affinity), fern leaves, tree trunks, and various kinds of plant pollen. What is rather strange, however, is that most of the fossil animals are typical marine creatures. What were they doing in a presumably freshwater river deposit? One answer is that these rivers were influenced by tremendous tidal bores. An analogous situation exists today in Australia on the Ord River where the incoming ocean tide can travel over forty miles upstream.

It's now too late in the day to continue any farther down into the canyon. But I can still get a close look at each layer. Back in Grand Canyon Village at the Bright Angel Lodge, the ten-foot high fireplace in the Fred Harvey Museum is constructed of rocks from each formation, starting with river-worn stones forming the hearth, to Kaibab Limestone surrounding the chimney.

Mountains, seas, deserts. Each layer of rock exposed in the walls of the Grand Canyon speaks of a different environment, a different habitat. The revered naturalist John Muir wrote, "The whole cañon is a mine of fossils . . . forming a grand geological library—a collection of stone books covering thousands of miles of shelving, tier on tier, conveniently arranged for the student."

I will come back again to read another page.

Overleaf: *View from Yavapai Point, looking east. (Photo © by Dick Dietrich.)*

First morning light and the full moon. (Photo © by Ron Sanford.)

CANYON ORIGINS

New York elevated-railway dispatcher William Wallace Bass came out to Arizona for his health in 1883. He got a job working for the Scott Ranch north of Williams along Cataract (Havasu) Canyon and lived for a time in a cave. One day he was out riding hard, chasing a little doggie—an orphaned calf, for you city dudes—through the pygmy forest near Rain Tanks. Suddenly, without any warning, the world just dropped away. Bass's startled horse reared up, throwing the cowboy to the ground. But Bass didn't notice the impact; he was reeling from the view. He had heard many tales about the Grand Canyon, but was still quite unprepared for his first encounter. He remarked, "It nearly scared me to death."

This apocryphal story illustrates one of the unique features of the canyon country: No matter from what direction you approach the Grand Canyon, there are few clues that an immense abyss is about to be encountered.

How did this wonderful gash in the earth come to be here, a canyon cut into a highland that averages over a mile above sea level? The traditional Havasupai tell the tale of Tochopa, a good, benevolent god, and Hokomata, an evil, mischievous deity. One day, Hokomata started a rainstorm that made a noise greater than a thousand Hackataias (the Colorado River). To save his daughter Pu-keh-eh from the flood, Tochopa put her in a hollowed-out pinyon log.

As the floodwaters rushed to the sea, the resulting force excavated Chic-a-mi-mi (the Grand Canyon). Pu-keh-eh crawled out of her makeshift boat unscathed and eventually became the progenitor of the human race.

Geologists tell a different story about the canyon's origin, a version not nearly as straightforward as the Havasupai's. The geologic story is fraught with contradictions, inconsistencies, and unresolved questions.

The Colorado River—the geologist's suspected agent in cutting the depth of the Grand Canyon—arrives out of Utah to the north through country considerably lower in altitude than the Kaibab Plateau. How did the river initially run up and over the higher plateau? And where did the river deposit all the excavated material, all that dirt?

John Wesley Powell wondered, too. During his historic first descent of the Green and Colorado Rivers in 1869, he noticed that at several locations the rivers had cut through uplifted plateaus such as Split Mountain, the Tavaputs, and the Kaibab. He postulated that at one time the ancestral Colorado River system flowed across a relatively level plain. When portions of the plain began to rise, these steeper gradients caused those lengths of the rivers to flow more swiftly and thus cut down faster. The rate of uplift did not exceed the rate of down-cutting, eventually developing the landscape that we see today. Like many other early geologists, Powell believed that the canyon was very old, perhaps fifty million years or more.

Powell's simple, elegant theory of the origin and age of the Grand Canyon was soon contradicted by geologist Clarence Dutton. "The most emphatic lesson that the canyon teaches is that it is not a very old feature of the earth's surface, but a very modern one; that it does not mark the accomplishment of a great task of earth sculpture, but only the beginning of such a task; and that in spite of its great dimensions, it is properly described as a young valley."

Neither Powell nor Dutton had any means to give absolute dates to the rocks and features they were describing and attempting to understand. Relative dating schemes could sometimes be worked out, provided that fossils were present and assuming that the layering of the rocks was still in its original order, with younger layers overlying older ones. Not until the early 1900s and the advent of radiometric dating—in which the known rate of decay of a radioactive isotope into a stable and is measured—could absolute dates be calculated.

During the 1930s and 1940s, research along the lower Colorado River and western Grand Canyon seemed to indicate that the landscape of this area was relatively young. For example, just west of the Grand Wash Cliffs, where the Colorado River emerges from the Grand Canyon, is the Muddy Creek Formation, which underlies the river's deposits. The Muddy Creek Formation has been radiometrically dated at six million years old, which implies that the Colorado River must be younger than six million years.

However, Powell believed—and current theory agrees—that the Kaibab Plateau began to rise during a mountain-building phase called the Laramide Orogeny some sixty-five million years ago. Since water usually doesn't flow uphill, how did the much younger Colorado cut through the already uplifted plateau?

In the 1960s, geologists studying the Marble Canyon segment of the Grand Canyon found evidence that seemed to indicate the river has been on its present course since at least the Oligocene epoch, or for about thirty million years. But if this section of the Colorado River is that old, where did it go for twenty-four million years before it flowed across the Muddy Creek Formation?

Additionally, geologists generally agree that the Gulf of California, location of the modern mouth of the river, didn't open up until four or five million years ago—a result of the tectonic "rafting" of the Baja peninsula away from the west coast of Mexico. So where did the Colorado River go for one or two million years after starting to flow across the Muddy Creek Formation?

A 1964 symposium convened by geologist Eddie McKee tried to make sense of all this conflicting data. The resulting hypothesis was that the ancestral Colorado River did indeed flow through Marble Canyon as it does today, but instead of turning to cut through the Kaibab Plateau, the river originally turned southeast to follow the present course of the Little Colorado River, perhaps reaching the Gulf of Mexico. Meanwhile, smaller tributary streams on either side of the Kaibab Plateau carved toward one another by a process known as headward erosion. When these streams met, the westerly flowing stream captured the drainage of the easterly flowing stream. The Colorado River was also captured at this confluence and began to flow west.

One major problem with this hypothesis, however, is that no one has discovered the ancestral Colorado's riverbed across eastern Arizona or New Mexico or Texas.

Ivo Lucchitta, a geologist for the United States Geological Survey (USGS) who has studied the Grand Canyon for over twenty-five years, has some new thoughts on the canyon's origin. "Powell and later geologists felt the river had an integral history. What was true of one part of the river was true of the whole thing. Abandoning simpler concepts, geologists are beginning to see rivers as evolving entities that adapt to environmental pressures much as biological systems develop."

Lucchitta's hypothesis begins with the ancestral Colorado following a course similar to today's, except in the vicinity of the present Grand Wash Cliffs and the western Grand Canyon. Here he believes the river flowed north or northwest into one of the great basins that existed prior to 5.5 million years ago in southwestern Utah and Nevada. The river flowed over the Kaibab Plateau before the plateau was exposed as a topographic feature by the erosion of the surrounding countryside. Thus the river did not encounter an uplift in its path. The ancestral Colorado and its load of "dirt" meandered off into the Great Basin of western Utah and Nevada. The Gulf of California opened, and a river draining into it, through the process of headward erosion, eventually captured the Colorado.

Lucchitta has also been studying river gravel deposits north of the Grand Canyon that could have come only from rock layers located south of the canyon. North-flowing streams, he concludes, must have transported and deposited these gravels prior to the Grand Canyon being carved. Some of these gravels are covered with basalt lavas that are six million years old. Lucchitta believes this evidence indicates that the present Colorado River course is less than 5.5 million years old and that the western Grand Canyon is only three to four million years old.

Don Elston, another USGS geologist, paints a slightly different picture. He too has studied the gravels north of the Grand Canyon, as well as gravel deposits west, southeast, and south of the canyon. He believes the evidence suggests a much longer period of erosion by the Colorado River, followed by a dry climatic period that reduced the river's flow and allowed the accumulation of the Muddy Creek Formation, which may have dammed the river. Around five million years ago, a climatic shift back to wetter conditions caused the Colorado to reestablish itself across the Muddy Creek Formation. Elston thus concludes that the canyon is about twelve million years old.

Other geologists disagree with both theories. Exactly how, when, and where all that dirt went will puzzle geologists for some time to come. In any case, the Grand Canyon is the culmination, the archetypal feature, of forces which created the physiographic region known as the Colorado Plateau. The plateau, covering 130,000 square miles of northern Arizona, southern Utah, western Colorado, and northwestern New Mexico, is a unique part of the earth. It is composed primarily of colorful sedimentary rocks that have been uplifted and then carved by the Colorado River and a myriad of tributaries into a labyrinth of canyons, mesas, buttes, spires, and arches.

After visiting the canyon at the turn of the century, the distinguished naturalist John Burroughs wrote: "Time, geologic time, looks out at us from the rocks as from no other objects in the landscape. Geologic time! How the striking of the great clock whose hours are millions of years, reverberates out of the abyss of the past! Mountains fall and the foundations shift as it beats out the moments of terrestrial history. Rocks have literally come down to us from a foreworld. The youth of the earth is in the soil and in the trees and verdure that spring from it; its age is in the rocks. . . . Even if we do not know our geology, there is something in the face of a cliff and in the look of a granite boulder that gives us pause."

I am struck by the ironic juxtaposition of knowing a great deal about each individual layer of rock—its origin, its physical makeup, its depositional environment and the creatures that lived there—while the details of the carving of these layers into the Grand Canyon still elude us. There is something satisfying in knowing that, despite all the scientific investigating and hypothesizing, unresolved mysteries of nature still abound.

Along the Salt Trail that leads from the Hopi Mesas to the Grand Canyon, the Hopi would often carve clan symbols to mark their passage. (Photo © by S. Aitchison.)

NATIVE AMERICANS

Strange night noises break my sleep. Must have been an owl. Then several small pebbles roll down the slope and fall next to my sleeping bag. Probably just a ringtail cat on the prowl. Do I hear drums? No, no, it's just the blood pounding in my ears. My rational side says to keep calm, but when I close my eyes, I see the handprint of Masau-u on the roof of a nearby cave.

Some Hopi say that Masau-u, kachina of the underworld, can manifest himself as a golden eagle, but the name *Masau-u* means "one who lives unseen," so his exact form is unknown. Yesterday, as we came down the rough route known as the Salt Trail, a golden eagle effortlessly drifted by us on a rising thermal. As the bird flew by, an unblinking eye stared at us. Despite the baking summer heat, I felt a chill.

Darkness had overtaken us before we reached the floor of this side canyon that leads to the Little Colorado River, and we were forced to camp not far from Masau-u's "home," a shallow cave marked by a handprint. I felt uneasy here, as though I were being watched. I remembered a story that I had heard about a hiker from New Zealand who had camped in the Little Colorado Gorge and was awakened during the night by someone playing a flute. Only later, back home, would the hiker learn about Kokopelli, the legendary flute player and trader of Hopi mythology, and ponder the strange encounter. During the previous winter, the *Navajo Times* had reported "something weird . . . roaming around the villages of First Mesa." Some traditional Hopi suspected it was Masau-u. Superstitious nonsense? Perhaps, but inexplicable things can happen in the desert.

I finally drifted off into a fitful sleep—from which I was soon to be awakened—dreaming about the next day's hike to the Sipapuni. To the geologist, the Sipapuni is an extraordinary, yellowish brown, dome-shaped, travertine spring deposit some twenty feet high and thirty feet in diameter, with a pool of ocher-colored, effervescing water at its summit. To the Hopi, this is the entrance to the underworld. Here the Hopi emerge into this world and return after death.

The Hopi, who today live amid three arid mesas east of the Grand Canyon, have revered the canyon for countless centuries and have legends explaining many of the canyon's formations. According to one legend, the War Twins and their grandmother, Spider Woman, proceeded westward from Third Mesa to prepare a trail leading good Hopi to a salt deposit. The twins turned Spider Woman to stone near the Grand Canyon after telling her, "Your private parts will show, and when Hopi pass, every man will get into you. In this way we will trade with each other, because, on their return, the Hopi will leave salt for you." (Apparently, the act of turning Spider Woman and others into stone accounts for the stone pillars and other rock formations that the Hopi rely upon as trail markers.)

The younger twin was turned to stone at the canyon rim so that the Hopi could find the trailhead. When the elder brother reached the home of Masau-u, he fortunately secured this powerful god's promise to help any Hopi who passed this way in the future. At the home of the kachina Koyemsi (Mudhead), he received a similar promise. Beside the Sipapuni, the elder twin said, "When salt gatherers come here, they will deposit their offerings and pray."

Finally reaching the Colorado River not far from its confluence with the Little Colorado, the elder twin walked along a ledge and rubbed his fists against the canyon walls. Everything he touched turned to salt. He then climbed up on a shelf above the salt and turned himself into a rock knob—a formation that has ever since assisted the Hopi in their descent to the salt mine.

The Hopi continued their physically challenging and spiritually dangerous salt trek until about 1912, when increasing contact with the Anglo-culture disrupted the regular pilgrimage. Occasional trips are still made today, but due to the sacredness of the area, the National Park Service has closed the salt mine to non-Hopi visitation.

When not in flood, this portion of the Little Colorado River is an incredible bluish white stream fed by springs, the largest being Blue Springs, located about thirteen miles upstream from the confluence with the main Colorado. Over ninety thousand gallons per minute gush out from a limestone overhang. The strange color is believed to be due to the refraction of light by water heavily mineralized by calcium carbonate and sodium chloride.

The ancestors of the Hopi—the yucca-sandaled Anasazi—and another similar group of people, the Cohonina, explored every corner of the canyon and its side-gorges. Some of their ancient routes, such as the one off Fossil Bay, require nearly technical rock-climbing skills. Even some of the great buttes and temples, such as Shiva

The Havasupai still live within a side canyon to the Grand, accessible only by trail or helicopter. Here the sacred Wigleeva rocks overlook their verdant valley. But all is not idyllic; the village suffered greatly from a terrible flash flood in 1990. (Photo © by Ralph Lee Hopkins, Wilderland Images.)

115

and Wotan, were scaled and small houses or storage rooms built near their summits. Most of the early trails were maintained simply through use, but in a few cases actual trail construction was performed. In Marble Canyon, for example, just a little upriver from President Harding Rapid, an Anasazi bridge is perched high in the Redwall Limestone. At first the bridge does not appear to lead to anywhere, but climbers have discovered a route continuing upward to the North Rim. (Due to the fragile nature of the bridge, the National Park Service requests that it be viewed only from a distance.) A route to the South Rim—the Eminence Break route also near President Harding Rapid—made a cross-canyon trip possible for these early canyon dwellers.

Of the several thousand known Anasazi and Cohonina ruins in the canyon, the vast majority date from A.D. 1050 to 1150. By examining the growth rings of trees growing during that time period, scientists have determined that the American Southwest experienced a century of slightly higher rainfall. This additional moisture apparently attracted the ancient farmers to what had been less than desirable areas for cultivation.

Yet the location of many of the Anasazi and Coconina ruins is puzzling. Fortlike structures were built on isolated pinnacles such as Wotan's Throne. Why so far from their crops? Furthermore, homesites along the South Rim are not near sources of drinking water. Where did the residents obtain water?

After a century of fairly intensive occupation, the people abandoned the canyon as a place to live, although ritualistic use of the area continued. Probably increasingly arid conditions made agriculture more tenuous in the already marginal farming environment. Perhaps other natural resources, such as firewood, had been seriously depleted.

Where did these people go? Most of the Anasazi were probably incorporated into the Hopi and other Pueblo cultures living to the east of the canyon. The fate of the Cohonina people is still unclear.

About two hundred years after the departure of the Anasazi and Cohonina, the Cerbat—who, according to some archaeologists, were the ancestors of the Hualapai and Havasupai—began to enter the canyon from the lower Colorado River valley. They spread as far east as the Little Colorado River, but stayed primarily south of the Colorado. They lived in circular brush wickiups and, instead of sandals, wore leather moccasins. During the winter, the Cerbat tended to stay along the rim where they could hunt for deer, rabbits, and other small game. In the spring, the people would move into the canyon near streams and springs and plant corn, beans, and squash. Today, the Hualapai Reservation includes the Grand Canyon south of the Colorado River and west of Havasu Canyon, but most of the inhabitants live in the community of Peach Springs straddling historic Route 66. Only the Havasupai continue to live within the canyon.

To learn a little more about these canyon people, my wife Ann and I planned a trip to their village, Supai, tucked in a deep side-canyon of the Grand Canyon. We thought this would also be a good opportunity to try our first overnight hike with our daughter, Kate—she was only eighteen months old and not much of a self-propelled hiker yet. From the parking area at Hualapai Hilltop to our destination at Supai Village is an eight-mile hike. To make life simpler (and our load lighter), we made reservations at the Havasupai Lodge, so at least we wouldn't have to carry sleeping bags and a tent.

Early March in the Grand Canyon can be "iffy" weatherwise. One day early-spring flowers such as globemallow and princess plume are budding out, but the next day winter's icy grip has frosted those foolish plants. Luckily, our chosen weekend was perfect for hiking.

I slipped on my backpack containing lunch, snacks, water, and other necessities of the trail. Ann carried Kate in a high-tech child carrier. I had offered to tote the little one, but Ann was suspicious of all the camera gear I was loading into my pack, and decided Kate was the lesser weight.

Hiking with kids, even one, and especially one strapped to your back, slows you down. In-

Near this spot the old Hopi Salt Trail descends into the Little Colorado River Gorge. (Photo © by S. Aitchison.)

Above: *Curtains of travertine near Mooney Falls suggest that the highly mineralized creek used to flow over this section of wall. (Photo © by S. Aitchison.)* **Below**: *Biologists carefully work their way down a treacherous route to Blue Springs in the Little Colorado River Gorge. (Photo © by S. Aitchison.)*

stead of pounding Vibram and making miles, we rested more often. Kate explored everything during these rest stops. Each rock, each plant became an exciting discovery. Through her untrained, unbiased, but very curious eyes, we saw nature and the world around us anew.

Midafternoon found us at the junction of Hualapai and Havasu canyons. Crystal clear Havasu Creek bubbles forth from springs a half-mile up Havasu Canyon. Another trail also comes from that direction, having started at a place called Topocoba Hilltop. Along that route in 1879, prospector Edward Doheny noted a drawing on the canyon wall that he thought resembled a dinosaur. Believing that dinosaurs must have still roamed the canyon when the first Indians arrived, he later sponsored an expedition to disprove Darwin's theory of evolution.

The 1924 Doheny Scientific Expedition found not only the famed dinosaur petroglyph, but also one that appeared to be an elephant attacking a man and another of an ibexlike creature. The director of the expedition, Samuel Hubbard, wrote, "The fact that some prehistoric man made a pictograph of a dinosaur on the walls of this canyon upsets completely all of our theories regarding the antiquity of man."

The "dinosaur" drawing, however, is hardly convincing, and the "ibex" is similar to other depictions of bighorn sheep, a very common subject for prehistoric Southwestern artists. The "elephant" petroglyph is indeed intriguing, considering that the earliest people on the Colorado Plateau hunted mammoths.

We soon turned to follow the creek downstream. Fences, irrigation ditches, and a simple plank bridge across the creek told us that we were approaching the village of Supai. A more idyllic setting would be hard to imagine—red cliffs tower above us, cottonwood trees adorned with fresh green leaves line a clear brook, pink blossoms explode on the numerous peach trees.

Below the village, the creek tumbles over a series of falls—Supai, Navajo, Havasu, and Mooney—each more spectacular than the last, and the water becomes an intense blue. As with the Little Colorado River, the color is due to dissolved minerals refracting the light. Aeration of the falling water causes certain minerals to precipitate out and enhances the refracting.

The name Havasupai, which is of Hualapai origin, is popularly translated as "the people of the blue-green waters." Ethnographer Alfred Whiting believes the meaning to be closer to "the people who live at the place which is green." Though it may not be as eloquent or romantic, this latter rendering is certainly appropriate, especially when one peers down upon the village on a summer day. Fields of corn, beans, and squash and groves of cottonwood, box elder, and willow produce a verdant patch within a red sandstone desert.

But life in this canyon is far from utopian. Isolation once helped to preserve the culture of the tiny Havasupai community, but today thousands of tourists visit their canyon home. The difficult clash of Native American and Anglo societies is clearly evident. Horses graze beneath television satellite dishes. A steady stream of helicopters fly in horse feed and other supplies. Aluminum cans, plastic bottles, and disposable diapers mar the landscape.

The contemporary native people of the Grand Canyon face an uncertain future. The rich diversity of cultures, like the biodiversity within an ecosystem, is what keeps the human spirit vibrant and dynamic. To become a monoculture is to risk becoming stagnant, decadent, and eventually extinct. As writer Wallace Stegner noted a half-century ago after trekking into Havasu Canyon, "The trail between . . . simple civilization and the inconceivably complex world beyond the rims is difficult even for those who can go at their own pace."

Lovely Havasu Falls in Havasu Canyon, not far downstream from Supai, the Havasupai's canyon home. (Photo © by S. Aitchison.)

The Big Dipper over the Grand Canyon on a winter's night. (Photo © by Vernon Eugene Grove Jr.)

SHRINKING WILDERNESS

I am about to fill out an application for a private river trip permit for the Colorado River through the Grand Canyon. This will put me on a waiting list, a wait of perhaps eleven—yes, eleven—years.

Gone are the days of just showing up at Lee's Ferry and setting off into the canyon wilderness. Today there are simply too many people wanting to do the same thing in the same place. I was involved in some of the early river studies that led to the present river management plan, so I am personally aware of the problems caused by unbridled recreation. But what happened to the wilderness experience?

Real wilderness—a wilderness so big that intrusion by humankind has no appreciable effect on the ecosystem—no longer exists. Our exploding population and modern technology have taken care of that. Wilderness today is more a mind-set than a physical reality. Those of us who enjoy the natural world pretend that our parks and wilderness areas are ecologically self-contained pristine islands. But nothing could be farther from the truth. To paraphrase the American naturalist John Muir, everything in the universe is hitched to something else.

Every time I learn about a new rule or required permit, the hairs on the back of my neck bristle. I think of a scene from the classic film *Treasure of the Sierra Madre* in which one character sneers, "Badges? I don't need no stinkin' badges."

But rules are a consequence of living in a supposedly civilized society. The National Park Service and other land-managing agencies have an extremely difficult balancing act—being stewards of the land yet allowing human activities, both recreational and commercial, to take place. Regulation seems to be an option, but too much regulation can destroy the sense of adventure, the thrill of the unknown, the essence of a true wilderness experience.

Ultimately, rules and permits alone will not save our wild places, our natural heritage. Only by learning to cherish the land and its inhabitants, to understand that we are part of nature not outside of it, to remember that our very survival is linked to the natural world—only by taking care of our delicate, fragile blue planet will humankind survive.

Will the earth care if we don't clean up our act or control our population growth? Does the Grand Canyon need us? Probably not. Humans will simply become extinct. Cyanobacteria—the blue-green algae whose billion-year-old fossils are found at the bottom of the Grand Canyon and still exist today—will probably continue on, but the couple-million-year history of humankind may become just a thin strata in the fossil record. Yet it's not too late to become a better neighbor in the natural community.

(Photo © by Dick Dietrich.)

FURTHER READING

Aitchison, Stewart. *A Naturalist's Guide to Hiking the Grand Canyon.* Prentice-Hall, Inc., Englewood Cliffs, NJ, 1985.

Armstrong, David. *Mammals of the Canyon Country.* Canyonlands Natural History Association, Moab, UT, 1982.

Brown, Bryan T., Steven W. Carothers, and R. Roy Johnson. *Grand Canyon Birds.* University of Arizona Press, Tucson, AZ, 1987.

Butchart, J. Harvey. *Grand Canyon Treks.* La Siesta Press, Glendale, CA, 1970.

Butchart, J. Harvey. *Grand Canyon Treks II.* La Siesta Press, Glendale, CA, 1975.

Butchart, J. Harvey. *Grand Canyon Treks III.* La Siesta Press, Glendale, CA, 1984.

Carrier, Jim. *Down the Colorado: Travels on a Western Waterway.* Roberts Rinehart, Inc. Publishers, Boulder, CO, 1989.

Collier, Michael. *An Introduction to Grand Canyon Geology.* Grand Canyon Natural History Association, Grand Canyon, AZ, 1980.

Crampton, C. Gregory. *Land of Living Rock: The Grand Canyon and the High Plateaus: Arizona, Utah, Nevada.* Alfred A. Knopf, New York, NY, 1972.

Crampton, C. Gregory, ed. *Sharlot Hall on the Arizona Strip: A Diary of a Journey Through Northern Arizona in 1911 by Sharlot Hall.* Northland Press, Flagstaff, AZ, 1975.

Dutton, Clarence. *Tertiary History of the Grand Canon District with Atlas.* U.S. Geological Survey Monographs, II. Government Printing Office, Washington, DC, 1882.

Easton, R., and M. Brown. *Lord of the Beasts—The Saga of Buffalo Jones.* University of Arizona Press, Tucson, AZ, 1961.

Evans, Edna. *Tales from the Grand Canyon.* Northland Press, Flagstaff, AZ, 1985.

Findley, Rowe. "Miracle of the Potholes." *National Geographic,* 148 (1975): 570–579.

Freeman, Lewis R. *The Colorado River: Yesterday, Today and To-morrow.* Dodd, Mead and Company, New York, NY, 1923.

Hirst, Stephen. *Havsuw 'Baaja: People of the Blue Green Water.* The Havasupai Tribe, Supai, AZ, 1985.

Hoffmeister, Donald F. *Mammals of the Grand Canyon.* University of Illinois Press, Urbana, IL, 1971.

Hughes, J. Donald. *In the House of Stone and Light.* Grand Canyon Natural History Association, Grand Canyon, AZ, 1978.

Hughes, J. Donald. *In the House of Stone and Light: A Human History of the Grand Canyon.* Grand Canyon Natural History Association, Grand Canyon, AZ, 1978.

Jaeger, Edmund C. *Desert Wildlife.* Stanford University Press, Stanford, CA, 1961.

James, George Wharton. *In and Around the Grand Canyon: the Grand Canyon of the Colorado River in Arizona.* Little, Brown, and Company, Boston, MA, 1900.

Jones, Anne Trinkle, and Robert C. Euler. *A Sketch of Grand Canyon Prehistory.* Grand Canyon Natural History Association, Grand Canyon, AZ, 1979.

Kirk, Ruth. *Desert: The American Southwest.* Houghton Mifflin Co., Boston, MA, 1973.

Krutch, Joseph Wood. *Grand Canyon: Today and all its yesterdays.* William Sloane Associates, Inc., New York, NY, 1957.

Lanner, Ronald M. *The Pinyon Pine: A Natural and Cultural History.* University of Nevada Press, Reno, NV, 1981.

Lavender, David. *River Runners of the Grand Canyon.* Grand Canyon Natural History Association and University of Arizona, Tucson, AZ, 1985.

Leopold, Aldo. *A Sand County Almanac*. Random House, New York, NY, 1966.

Loving, Nancy J. *Along the Rim: A Road Guide to the South Rim of Grand Canyon*. Grand Canyon Natural History Association, Grand Canyon, AZ, 1981.

Lucchitta, Ivo. "Canyon Maker—The Geological History of the Colorado River." *Plateau*, Museum of Northern Arizona, 59 (1988).

MacMahon, James A., ed. *Desert*. Alfred A. Knopf, Inc., New York, NY, 1985.

Martin, Russell. *A Story That Stands Like a Dam: Glen Canyon and the Struggle for the Soul of the West*. Henry Holt, New York, NY, 1989.

Miller, D. M., R. A. Young, T. W. Gatlin, and J. A. Richardson. *Amphibians and Reptiles of the Grand Canyon*. Grand Canyon Natural History Association, Monograph No. 4, Grand Canyon, AZ, 1982.

Nabhan, Gary Paul. *Gathering the Desert*. University of Arizona Press, Tucson, AZ, 1985.

Peattie, Roderick, ed. *The Inverted Mountains: Canyons of the West*. The Vanguard Press, Inc., New York, NY, 1948.

Phillips, Arthur M. *Grand Canyon Wildflowers*. Grand Canyon Natural History Association, Grand Canyon, AZ, 1979.

Powell, John Wesley. *The Exploration of the Colorado River and its Canyons*. 1895. Reprint. Dover Publications, Inc., New York, NY, 1961.

Redfern, Ron. *Corridors of Time*. Orbis Publishing Limited, London, England, 1980.

Russo, John P. "The Kaibab North Deer Herd: Its History, Problems, and Management." *Wildlife Bulletin ;7*, Arizona Game and Fish Department, Phoenix, AZ, 1964.

Schwartz, Douglas W. "On the Edge of Splendor: Exploring Grand Canyon's Human Past." *Exploration: The Annual Bulletin of the School of American Research*, Sante Fe, NM, 1990.

Shankland, Robert. *Steve Mather of the National Parks*. Alfred A. Knopf, New York, NY, 1951.

Simmons, Leo W., ed. *Sun Chief, the Autobiography of a Hopi Indian*. Yale University Press, New Haven, CN, 1942.

Spamer, Earle E., comp. *Bibliography of the Grand Canyon and the Colorado River: 1540–1980*. Grand Canyon Natural History Association, Monograph Number 2, Grand Canyon, AZ, 1981.

Stegner, Wallace. *The Sound of Mountain Water*. Doubleday & Company, Inc., Garden City, NY, 1969.

Sterling, K. B. *Last of the Naturalists—The Career of C. Hart Merriam*. Arno Press, New York, NY, 1974.

Stevens, Larry. *The Colorado River in Grand Canyon: A Guide*. Red Lake Books, Flagstaff, AZ, 1983.

Thayer, Dave. *A Guide to Grand Canyon Geology Along the Bright Angel Trail*. Grand Canyon Natural History Association, Grand Canyon, AZ, 1986.

Thybony, Scott. *A Guide to Hiking the Inner Canyon*. Grand Canyon Natural History Association, Grand Canyon, AZ, 1980.

Whitney, Stephen. *A Field Guide to the Grand Canyon*. William Morrow and Company, Inc., New York, NY, 1982.

ACKNOWLEDGMENTS

Many people have generously shared with me their special knowledge about the Grand Canyon. Sometimes I listened and learned; other times I stubbornly held on to my own prejudices. In either case, I owe them a great deal of thanks.

A few of these folks are Jan Balsom, George Bain, George Billingsley, Douglas Brown, Stanley Beus, Steve Carothers, Polly Hays, Martos Hoffman, Bill Leibfried, Jim Mead, Julie Roller, Jim Ruch, Larry Stevens, and Scott Thybony.

Writers wouldn't get very far without libraries. I would like to thank John Irwin and staff of the Flagstaff Public Library, Dotty House of the Museum of Northern Arizona Library, the staff of the Northern Arizona University Library, William Mullane of NAU's Special Collections, and Valerie Meyer of the Grand Canyon National Park Research Library

for their help.

Thanks also to Dick Dietrich and the other fine photographers who provided the outstanding images used in the book. My only regret is that I wished I could have used more of the photos.

For critically reviewing the manuscript I am in debt to John Davis, Superintendent of Grand Canyon National Park, Douglas Brown, National Park Service Resources Management Specialist at Grand Canyon, my friend David Maren, and my wife, Ann. Lisa Oelfke had the onerous task of shoring up my syntax and polishing my grammar. Any uncited opinions or errors of fact are strictly my own.

And finally, I want to thank Bob DuBois for suggesting this writing project, and Helene Jones, Kathy Mallien, and the rest of the staff of Voyageur Press for putting it all together.

ABOUT THE AUTHOR

Naturalist and photographer Stewart Aitchison has been exploring the Grand Canyon region for over twenty-five years. He escorts natural history trips for Lindblad's Special Expeditions on the Colorado Plateau, Southeast Alaska, and Baja California. He is a member of The Authors Guild, Inc. and has written other books about the American Southwest, including *A Guide to Exploring Oak Creek and the Sedona Area, A Hiker's Guide to Arizona* (with Bruce Grubbs), *A Naturalist's San Juan River Guide, A Naturalist's Guide to Hiking the Grand Canyon,* and *Utah Wildlands.* He makes his home with his wife Ann and daughter Kate in Flagstaff just a short drive south of the Grand Canyon.